AF574428

Visits to the Manger

Visits to the Manger

Enlightening Parables of Spiritual Wonder

Robert Chaney

Published by

792 W. Arrow Highway
Upland, CA 91786

Books by the Author

Akashic Records: Past Lives and New Directions

The Power of Your Own Medicine

Ten Steps to Self Fulfillment

The Inner Way

Mysticism—The Journey Within

The Essenes and Their Ancient Mysteries

Unfolding the Third Eye

Think on New Levels

The Jeweled Tree of Life

Occult Hypnotism

Reincarnation: Cycle of Opportunity

Transmutation: How the Alchemists
Turned Lead into Gold

❖

Cover By:
Robert Howard

Library of Congress
Catalogue Card
#96-083970

ISBN #0-918936-32-2

Printed in the United States of America

Acknowledgements

Editing and production assistance in publishing this book is gratefully acknowledged by the author. Contributions by the following associates and family are beyond measurement or description.

Earlyne and Sita Chaney, Pamela Rau, Jeffrey Meyer, Steve Doolittle and Beth Hickerson.

I thank each of you for your interest, your ideas, and your professional planning and guidance.

Dedication

Our daughter, Sita Chaney, spent half her life urging me to write this book. Therefore it is dedicated to her with love, admiration and gratitude.

Table of Contents

"...open the way for spiritual meaning to find an objective reality in your mind, in your heart and in your life."

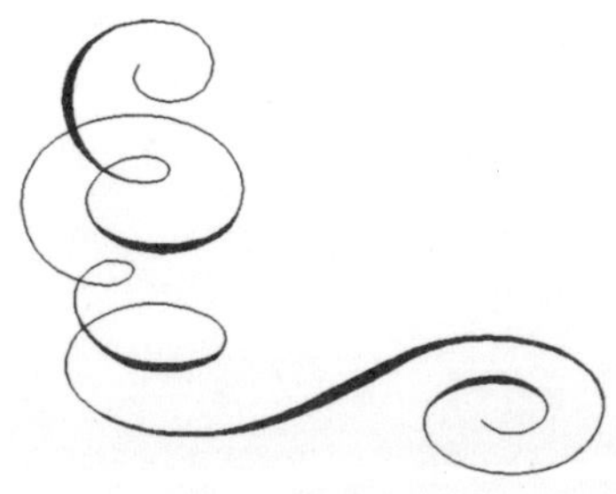

Prologue

Jesus was a storyteller. "A sower went forth to sow..." "Two men went to the temple to pray..." "There was a judge in a city..." He told simple but moving stories which continue to inspire us. They reveal our own potentials through the symbolism of fictional narratives with a spiritual focus.

Now, two thousand years removed from his unsurpassed skills with spiritual parables, I've attempted to create, through stories, an inner mode of consciousness that may help *you* recapture the spirit of *his* time, and encourage the spiritual focus of our time. I hope you find in these pages a way to taste the flavor of miracles, experience the presence of angels, perhaps even to fulfill some of your needs and aspirations. What a wonderful result that would be for both of us.

The birth of Jesus as historically chronicled was an event that obviously changed the world. It gave humankind a perspective on the meaning and value of life that has since been subject to innumerable interpretations, each of them sustaining the specific views of those who accepted it.

For conventional Christianity it's a time of joy, as any birth should be. For some it's a birth of God in human form, as his own son...a process that was common to many pre-Christian traditions and mythologies. For others, it was a reality-symbol of the idea that, along with the human spirit, the Divine spirit is embodied in every birth.

But aside from any historical or mythological meaning of the Birth, and the joyous celebratory method of commemorating it, is there some way of achieving a personal significance attached to the event, meaningful to each individual who accepts it? I think so.

Each of these stories was created for the purpose of helping you experience the event in the most personal, individual, meaningful way possible. Each story attempts to open the way for spiritual meaning to find an objective reality in your mind, in your heart and in your life.

Each story contains a special group of circumstances which are, in themselves, contemporary with situations in modern everyday life. Perhaps some of them mirror the unique grouping of conditions in your life. If so, they will help you connect with the Nativity narrative in a personal inner way not usually included in Christmas observances.

Each story includes some form of visit to the historical manger, and an exchange of gifts with the Christ Child. The symbolism of the literary device pertains to the actual interchange of energy between you and the higher, Divine dimensions of life. It's intended to be a form of personal inner birth experience. And the objective reality of the experience is that you can, if you wish, apply or direct that energy, through the words of the story, to benefit, heal or transform the actual circumstances of your life today.

In connecting with the personality or the experience of any character you select in each story, you may find a new birth in your own life. Each time that experience occurs, both you and the author are rewarded with a gift beyond price.

Robert Chaney
Upland, California

"...there's more than one way to follow a star..."

The Night There Was No Star

There was a man name Geshem, an Arabian who lived a distance of 300 or more stadia south of Bethlehem. (That's about 80 miles in our distance.) He was anything but a pleasant fellow, and probably had never entertained a spiritual thought during the entire 35 years of his life. His earliest childhood wasn't even a faint memory. Later, he could recall being hungry until he was about 15, though the passing years had never been counted, for he knew neither the when nor where of his birth.

Throughout his youth Geshem had fought for food, and sometimes even as little as a drink of water. He was cynical and calloused. For years he had found menial work caring for caravan camels that occasionally rested overnight in the small village near the caves of Engedi where he had spent his entire life. He learned that by taking good care of the mangy beasts he earned an extra lepton or two. (Each lepton was worth about one-eighth of a cent in our money.) By listening carefully to the caravan masters as they talked around the dim night fires, he acquired, over the years, a knowledge of desert lore and a cunning type of business sense. He firmly promised himself, over and over, that he would become wealthy.

"Rich!" he would often say, "That's what I intend to be, and I *will* be."

So he learned how to bargain. How to hide defects in goods as well as in sheep, donkeys and camels, so unsuspecting purchasers would pay higher prices for them. How to take advantage of others at every opportunity. How to buy low and sell high. Finally, after years of meager earnings, he acquired enough money to purchase his own camel. He then set his mind on obtaining a few carpets to offer for sale in Tekoah, the nearest village with a marketplace on the road to Bethlehem.

One early morning, three strange and obviously wealthy travelers entrusted him with their camels to be fed, watered and rested during the day. They explained they had traveled from dusk to dawn. As he removed their saddles he was filled with envy at the luxurious leather, workmanship and fastenings, and he realized these were persons of importance and wealth from whom he might learn a great deal.

He decided, therefore, to listen closely to their conversations. It was difficult, for the strangers kept quite to themselves. However, he did hear them speak of a magical star they were following, which explained why they traveled at night rather than in the cool early morning and late afternoon hours of daylight, as did most travelers. They expressed their faith in the magical star which, they said, was leading them nearer their king.

Throughout the day Geshem thought about the star and the possibility of being led to a king. "A king," he reasoned, "would surely pay handsomely for some beautiful carpets."

Shortly after midday he took a bold step toward his goal of wealth. He purchased two superb carpets handwoven by a local family, totally consuming his savings, but he knew he would turn a handsome profit on their sale to the king who the strangers discussed. He planned to follow them through the night and hopefully gain the king's personal attention.

As dusk was falling, he prepared the strangers' camels for their journey. He shuddered occasionally as the piercing chill of the desert night penetrated the folds of his galabeya. The peculiar foreigners mounted their camels and disappeared into the dusk as he began to roll and load his precious but heavy carpets on his own camel. It took much longer than he thought, and he was concerned that the strangers must have traveled several stadia before he was ready to follow. However he noticed that, just as they had said, an unusually bright star appeared in a peculiar location to the north. He reasoned that it must be the one the strangers discussed, so he urged his camel in that direction.

All night he followed the light in the sky. He never caught sight of the three uncommon travelers, but he believed they must have passed that way. He rested most of the next day, ate a meager meal of dried figs and dates, and slept a fitful sleep. That evening he took up the journey again, following the star.

The night chill seemed even colder than usual, and after traveling a few stadia, a wind from the north began blowing the sand in swirls. With swiftly increasing ferocity it stung his flesh and blinded his eyes. The brightness of the star decreased as the swirling sand increased. In the distance he saw dimly what seemed to be a small oasis, and he struggled to reach it before the now roaring sandstorm engulfed him completely. There was no longer a star—only the black night filled with churning pellets of fury.

In the darkness, Geshem stumbled into a small palm that was bent nearly double in the wind. He was momentarily startled by what he thought to be a little animal also seeking shelter. Suddenly, to his astonishment, he heard a child's voice, a small girl, crying a plaintive, pitiful whimper of hunger, pain and fear. Seeking his own safety from the storm, Geshem ignored her desperate cries for a time. Then he realized that without help and shelter the frightened little youngster would surely die.

Staggering from the force of the wind he unloaded his precious carpets from the camel, knelt down beside her, and covered them both with the carpets to protect against the ferocious storm. He sensed that the quivering little body beside him had begun to relax, and in spite of the roaring wind was soon asleep.

As the storm continued to bury them in the sand, his own feelings were mingled, full of questions. "Will I ever find the three strangers again? What happened to the star? Will I ever see it again?

"What about my precious carpets, now covered with sand, many of their delicate strands cut to shreds by the sandy grit? What about my investment, now in ruins along with the carpets?

"But, what would have happened to the child had I not accidentally found her? Was it really an accident?"

At what he thought was about the midnight watch, the violent winds began to calm. The sky was pitch black overhead, but still there was no star. "I've lost my gamble for a huge profit," he lamented, but for some reason he seemed slightly resigned, almost indifferent about it. He then fell into a troubled sleep—a dreamflight—even more unusual than his sand-swept search for riches.

In his strange, mystical vision, Geshem found himself in a village filled with people, travelers from afar as well as local townspeople. He seemed to float among them for a time, then drifted away from the crowded streets to a stable behind an inn—and there he encountered an unusual sight. Among others in the stable were the three strangers whose camels he had attended. But what a disappointment—there was no king.

He watched closely as everyone present approached the manger, but he couldn't see inside—and he wondered why some knelt and seemed to pray. Some, like the three strangers, apparently left a token. He noticed something odd about all of them—that when they turned to leave there was a peculiar incandescence aglow in their features, as if they had by some means begun to shine like a star in the dark of night.

As his dream continued, he decided he would see for himself what it was in the manger that had the power to cause such changes in the appearance of those who approached it. So he made his way forward. A step or so from the manger he was startled to discover it was occupied by a baby.

Entranced now, he looked into the eyes of the Child. "There's a star in each of them," he exclaimed to himself as he became aware of a twinkling gleam that flowed to him from the Babe.

Words leaped into his mind. It was as though the newly born infant himself was speaking them. "You have helped one of the least in all the desert, and I know of it."

* * * * * * *

Let's pause at this point in our story to engage in a moment of spiritual reverie...a meditation guided to the time and place of The Birth.

As you become at ease in your present surroundings, sense that your consciousness is flowing to that Great Moment of so long ago. The awesome moment of expectancy fulfilled is taken into your being with every breath.

The thoughts in your mind are the same as those in the minds of the shepherds, the Wise Men, the townspeople: "I am participating in a cosmic miracle—the conscious birth of the Christ Spirit in physical form...in the person of the Babe, but also in me and every person who accepts it."

After reflecting upon this event, and feeling and becoming responsive to its energies, let the focus of your consciousness return to these pages, to Geshem, and the lost waif he befriended.

* * * * * * *

At that moment Geshem's dream slowly faded and he awakened to find the little girl at his side touching his shoulder. Nearly overcome by his own dejection, he turned away from her.

"My poor carpets," was his immediate, distressed thought. "They're beyond repair, choked with sand, unfit for sale."

Suddenly he heard the hysterical shrieks of a woman crying, "There's my child! There she is!"

And the child's response, "Mama, Mama! Look Mama, this man saved my life last night when I lost my way in the storm."

"Thanks...thanks to God," stammered the woman, and through a flow of joyful tears she invited Geshem to her barren home, one of perhaps six or seven clustered nearby under a few palms in what couldn't even be called a village.

In the woman's home he witnessed the poverty of the family with no husband, yet he saw love there too. He suddenly had the urge to help in some way, but he had nothing to give save the worthless carpets. He offered them to the mother who accepted them gladly, for they were precious to her in spite of being valueless in the marketplace. For a time Geshem pondered this paradox, and recalling his dream, impressed him to think of it as a higher kind of lesson than those he'd been learning at the caravan campfires.

He realized it was pointless for him to continue his journey. So he saddled his camel, mounted, and turned homeward. But he felt that in some way he wasn't the same person who was so anxious to sell carpets to a king for a huge profit. He still continued to think about the star, too, but he had the peculiar feeling that it wasn't in the sky; it was in *him*.

After a long period of deep wonderment and thoughtfulness, he said to himself, "There must be more than one way to follow a star. Perhaps it's inside you—wherever you go." How true! How true!

So, as you come to the close of this story, meditate a few moments on your own inner star. Let it shine, and shine, and shine upon all the world.

Be reminded that in the great journey of life it is more important to gain inner riches than outer. That life is full of inner awakenings which, after all, are new births. And that even though it isn't always visible, there's more than one way to follow a star—and, whether it can be seen or not, no night is ever without one.

"Briefly they were one—united by that eloquent but fleeting glance with which prospective mothers silently say so much to each other."

The Christmas Birthmark

The man blocking the doorway of the inn was shouting, "There's no room I tell you! No room!"

The traveler, who had said his name was Joseph, turned away, head bowed in disappointment. He led a donkey and rider toward a cattle pen, a short distance behind the inn. Through taut lips the innkeeper exhaled a long sigh of relief.

He continued to think about the situation as he viewed it. The beautiful though very young woman seated upon the donkey was obviously with child. The man Joseph was undoubtedly old enough to be her father, yet seemed as attentive as a newly wed husband.

Still standing in the doorway, reflecting on his good fortune at being rid of the unwelcome travelers, the innkeeper muttered to himself, "Something strange going on there. That older man and young woman. My inn has too good a reputation to get involved."

The long string of implications, which the situation fostered in the innkeeper's mind, furthered his belief that he had made the right decision in turning the travelers away, even though he actually did have rooms available. He wanted no discredit upon his inn, especially when so many wealthy patrons and free-spending government officials were about. Pleased with himself at his good business judgment, he turned, went inside, and closed the door. Joseph led the donkey carrying Mary slowly and carefully through the jostling crowd toward the manger.

An elaborate entourage, approaching the inn, blocked their way and trapped them motionless a few moments against the building's wall. In the center of the caravan a luxurious, covered and curtained portable couch paused alongside the donkey. From inside a woman partially parted the curtains. She, too, was with child. Her eyes met Mary's in a fleeting but meaningful encounter. Briefly they were one—united by that eloquent but fleeting glance with which prospective mothers silently say so much to each other.

The encounter was quickly interrupted as the couch suddenly lurched forward. But the moment lingered with Mary. She raised her hand, indicating to Joseph that she preferred not to hurry on, but to continue watching the caravan as it passed slowly through the crowded, narrow street. For some reason a mystical fascination beyond the sharing of motherhood held her attention, and her interest. It was as though the brief meeting established a tie that was to have further consequences at a later time. She experienced that peculiar sensation of being joyful but at the same time troubled.

Mary and Joseph observed that the caravan stopped at the inn, and was received with obvious relish by the innkeeper. They were given beautiful accommodations befitting travelers who arrive with a lavish retinue, compared to those whose caravan consists of a single donkey.

Not long afterwards, both Mary and the wealthy woman, whose name was Damaris, gave birth to their children. As the days passed, well-wishers arrived to visit both families. In love, awe and admiration, shepherds and the poor brought gifts to Mary and her child. Damaris and her child were visited by those who brought congratulations as a greedy, flimsy veil for the selfish gifts and favors they really sought for themselves. Unknown to Damaris, a dreadful event was in the making.

First, a curious birthmark appeared on her son's forehead. It was in the shape of a cross, the kind upon which criminals were often executed. Then, to her further dismay, she discovered that her son's world was totally dark. He was blind. Flashing baubles held before his face caused no response from his sightless eyes. Nevertheless she loved him dearly and held him closer as if to love away his misfortune.

Her neighbor was unable to interpret the dream. And Keturah refused to speak of it to her worthless, scornful, heartless husband. He hardly provided for her, and he cared not at all about her wish for a child. He obtained occasional menial employment at the inn, and of course he was well aware of the wealthy woman guest, and the birth of her child. He learned from a chambermaid that the child was blind. In his twisted mind he now beheld a rare opportunity and conceived an evil plan. He would steal the wealthy woman's baby and give him to Keturah, telling her the child was not wanted by his parents. Then he would report Keturah to the authorities, and thereby rid himself of her and at the same time receive a reward from the child's wealthy parents. Spurred by the possibility of great gain, he lost no time putting his plan into action.

Damaris and her son were both asleep that night as he entered her room. The fates were with him, he reasoned. Ever so quietly he lifted the babe from his bed, left the inn by the rear door and headed for his shack to give the child to Keturah. On the outskirts of the town he encountered three men who were riding their camels so swiftly they paid no heed to him as he cowered in the shadows.

* * * * * * *

We know, of course, they were the three Wise Men who came to pay their homage to the Christ Child at the manger. Let's join them in a meditation.

As I stand in the presence of a vital incarnation of the One Great Spirit, I sense that same Presence in myself now.

It brings new life to my own mind and spirit. It gives new birth to vital energies throughout my entire being.

I am spiritually blessed by this experience, lifted indeed to a new and higher level of life expression.

I sense that this functional merging of the Great Spirit with my spirit leads to the birth of new and challenging circumstances in my life, so I stand ready to accept them and through them to become more than I am now.

* * * * * * *

Keturah's husband placed the stolen babe in her surprised but eager arms and gave her his false explanation. Then he hurriedly left to carry out the next step in his evil plan, reporting to the authorities that *she* had kidnapped the child.

Keturah was overjoyed at the cuddling infant in her arms. She was so anxious for a child of her own that she unhesitatingly accepted her husband's story that the parents did not want the baby due to his blindness. Her neighbor, who came to share in Keturah's joy, then made a suggestion based upon other remarkable events in the town.

"Why do you not take the child to the stable close by the inn?" she asked. "The lame, and even the blind, are being healed as they come into the presence of the mother and Child who are always surrounded by a glowing light."

Keturah wondered if such a miracle might actually happen, and she determined to find out. Quickly she wrapped the child in a warm blanket and left straightway for the stable. Thus, unknown to her, a miracle was already accomplished, for by leaving her home she avoided the arrest which her husband had so wickedly planned.

As she arrived at the stable, three imposing figures were just leaving. Two of them mounted their camels, but the third approached Keturah, smiled gently, and lightly touched the baby's tiny head.

"Enter," he said, nodding toward the manger, "and you will be blessed even as we have been."

Keturah seemed transported to some unimaginable realm, an utterly incomprehensible state of mind, as she entered the manger area. The light...it seemed to welcome her. The unspoken attitude of others already present...it seemed to embrace her. The very air itself...it seemed to stir an inner nobleness, as though she could willingly make any sacrifice on behalf of the child she held in her arms.

She knelt beside another woman. And in a moment noticed the woman was crying softly. After a time there was a sudden stirring in the crib. The light surrounding it seemed to glow even brighter. The Child slightly raised one of his tiny hands, then his eyes looked directly at the sobbing woman kneeling beside Keturah. At this, she slowed her tears and spoke, her halting words interrupted by frequent sobs.

"Thou art such a babe," she said, "that I cannot imagine your having the power to grant a plea—especially from as unworthy a one as I am. But if it *is* possible—I ask that my baby son be returned. He is blind. And there is a birthmark on his forehead by which I shall recognize him if ever I see him again." She ceased speaking, silent tears trickling down her cheeks.

Keturah immediately realized whose child was cuddled in her arms. She remembered her dream that she had held in her arms a child which was hers and yet was not, and was suddenly stricken numb that she might have to give him up. She wanted so to keep him. She imagined what the years would be like, their romping together on the sunny hillsides, her teaching him to be good and strong. His growing to proud manhood. And perhaps one day he could be a merchant, or an innkeeper.

Even as these happy thoughts tumbled through her mind, she knew they could not be. Suddenly she became aware that the eyes of the Babe in the crib were directly upon her. It seemed almost as if they entered her own consciousness—and with them she saw the child raised to manhood with his real mother. Then, as the vision faded, even though she knew the child was not to be hers, she prayed.

"Just as there is love in this child's heart, let there also be light in his eyes," she implored.

She turned to Damaris, and lifted back the coverlet over the baby's forehead, revealing the birthmark to the startled, speechless mother. At that moment both women stared in astonishment as the birthmark slowly faded away, dissolved perhaps by the marvelous alchemy of a shared love.

As the two women looked into the child's face, his eyes slowly opened. He looked first toward Keturah, raised his hand and softly touched her cheek, as if to say, "Thank you." Then he turned his head toward the other Babe for a moment. A curious, soft glow of light surrounded them both. And finally he turned to his mother; the wrinkle of a first smile caressed his lips. He snuggled against her breast and fell asleep.

The two women stared at each other in amazement. They both knew that by some remarkable miracle the child was no longer blind. Together they turned to look at The Other Child in the crib—and somehow they felt that he knew it too.

"...if we will think of the qualities we need most, we will find them within the manger of our hearts..."

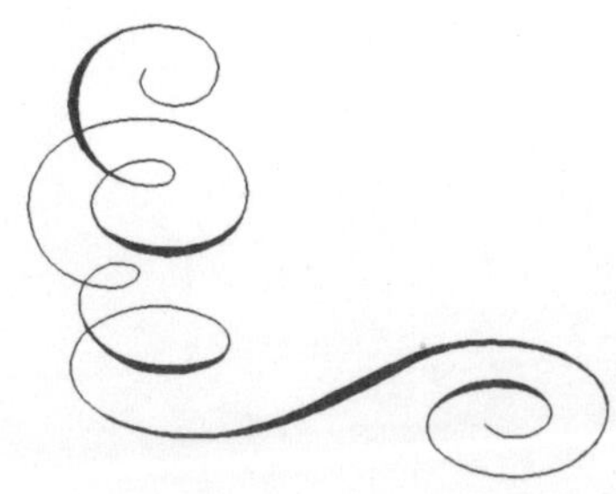

In the Days of Herod

Once upon a long, long time ago—in the days of Herod, king of Jerusalem, when the Babe lay in the manger at Bethlehem—thousands of miles away from that holy place there lived an extraordinary man. This is, in part, his story.

He lived in the area described by Longfellow in the epic poem *Hiawatha*, "By the shores of Gitche Gumee, by the shining Big-Sea-Water"—the place that you and I know today as Lake Superior. He was an old Ojibwa medicine man, highly respected by his own and the neighboring tribes. Tarawah was his name. Many came to his wigwam from afar to be healed, to receive his blessing upon their important ventures, and to consult with him regarding their problems.

He was considered *kiwanee* which, in some Indian dialects, means to be a little bit crazy. Now this is not crazy in the common sense of insanity—far from it. It means that his consciousness was often focused upon a vibratory realm not usually or readily available to the rest of us. Matters that entered his vision and his mind were often outside the comprehension of all who admired him, and who believed that his being kiwanee made him superior in that special wisdom which is beyond normal understanding.

One morning at sunrise in Ojibwa land, which was nightfall in Bethlehem, Tarawah fell into a deep sleep after an all night meditation vigil. However it wasn't the sleep of the weary warrior or hunter, but the sleep or trance that allowed him to slip away from his body and travel through the skies to another place.

He had done this often, but never had he traveled so far away—across plains and mountains, and a sea larger than he had ever seen. He found himself in a strange land, and among strange people who spoke a dialect he had never heard. Even so, miraculously he understood their thoughts. He found himself in a place where apparently a special birth had occurred. He was one of the first to arrive after the event, and he wondered why in the name of the Great Spirit he had been attracted to this peculiar place, for it was not of his asking.

One by one a few women arrived. They spoke in awed, hushed voices among themselves. And very timidly they spoke to the one who seemed to be the mother of the infant. Tarawah quickly realized he was not visible to any of them, although the mother once looked toward him for a long moment and a knowing kind of smile danced and glowed upon her face. He felt sure she had seen him, and he felt comfortable about it.

"If she lived among the Ojibwas, she would be kiwanee too. And even the papoose," he thought, "has a special destiny—and probably also is kiwanee. Perhaps one day he may come to Gitche Gumee and will honor my wigwam and my people by his presence."

The women spoke about the beauty of the Babe, the peacefulness of the mother, and the special caring expressed by the older man present.

"The Babe will lead us to peace," said one of the women as she and her friends left gifts of beautifully handcrafted clothing for the Child.

Tarawah became certain of his opinion that the Babe was kiwanee as other women also left gifts, for as each gift was presented the Child raised his hand as if recognizing the thoughts of the giver.

Later, as darkness hid the sky, several men arrived. They, too, seemed awed. But their remarks differed from those of the women.

"He will free us," one of them said. "No more Roman rule. He is the Saviour."

The men's conversations were more agitated and less subdued than the women's. They spoke of the oppressive taxes, of limitations on their freedom, of those who had been made slaves and sent to the ships or mines to toil unto death, all at the command of Herod the king.

Tarawah sensed that these men were from the nearby hillsides, and his intuition was confirmed when they exchanged views about the signs and voices in the heavens which they had seen and heard. They too left gifts—trinkets made from simple materials, tiny sandals of reeds, colored wooden balls for the Child to grasp and develop his muscles, an animal skin belt. At each gift, again, the tiny hand raised in recognition and acknowledgment of the thought behind it.

A few days and nights sped quickly by, for Tarawah's consciousness mode was outside the limits of time. A steady stream of visitors passed through the area. Some wept. Others prayed. Some brought gifts and others did not. But always there was a change in their demeanor as the little hand raised, and the little eyes twinkled, in recognition of each person.

Tarawah sat for a long time in meditation, inwardly reviewing the invisible factors influencing the place and circumstances of the odd land and people around him. How different it was from his homeland. He became aware of kingly despots, greedy for land and gold. Of priestly oppressors, hungry for position and power. He realized there are always greedy Herods and hungry priests whose days must sooner or later come to an end. And he realized that in the Babe before him was the pure potential for bringing a state of greater enlightenment into existence.

Once, Tarawah's attention was specially aroused by a surprised gasp from those present at the moment. Three magnificently garbed men entered the circle of light. A hush fell upon the rest of the gathering as the men approached the crib. There was a long silence and it seemed to Tarawah that the Great Spirit was more than ever present. Finally one of the men spoke.

"He will give us faith," he said. Then he placed a small packet, or pouch, beside the crib.

After a few moments the second said, "He will give us hope." He, too, stepped forward and left a small pouch.

Another pause filled with the energy of hushed anticipation, then the third spoke. "He will give us love." His pouch also was placed beside the Babe.

Tarawah was filled with an overwhelming urge to join the three strange chiefs (to him that is what they appeared to be). It was as though a great spirit filled him and prompted him to move forward to the crib also. But, he hesitated for he had no gift to present.

Then a totally unexpected miracle occurred. In his ethereal hands he felt the physical presence of the medicine pouch that had been his prized possession throughout most of his life. Using the stones, crystals and feathers it contained, he had made good medicine for all who came to him in need. Without even questioning the miracle of it, he withdrew from the medicine pouch the most prized item of them all—a healing gemstone. Without hesitation he stepped to the crib, still invisible to all but the three Wise Men, and offered the gemstone to the little hand which quickly grasped it.

* * * * * * *

> You may wish to join the Wise Men and Tarawah at the crib through the meditative use of your inner faculty of creative imaging. Use your inner capacity for visualization to carry you back through space and time as did Tarawah. See the scene in its soft light from the dim oil lamp, sense the atmosphere of peace, harmony, love and...Presence.
>
> If, in your meditation, you will look upon the gemstone from Tarawah's medicine pouch for a moment, I will tell you its meaning.

* * * * * * *

The gemstone had been given to Tarawah by his father, a great medicine man who taught him the wise lore of the shamans. Tarawah treasured the stone above all his possessions. He had worn it smooth from years of handling it in the service of others. Its meaning is contained in the stone itself and in its swirling colors.

The stone represents a person. Its inner energies are like a human spirit incarnate in solid physical form, bearing within all the inherent power of the One Great Spirit.

The brown colors symbolize the problems and illnesses that become entwined in every lifetime. The white is for the presence of the eternal spirit within each human being. The pink shows how the mixture of faith and hope and love with the inner spirit becomes an agent of healing.

But there's another ingredient, an invisible one, signified by the significant words Tarawah spoke as he stood before the crib.

"He will give us understanding," he said.

Then he slowly turned away and began his mystical journey, back to Gitche Gumee and his wigwam by the Shining-Big-Sea-Water.

What did the wise old medicine man mean by his remark? It was spoken as a prophecy—"He will give us understanding."

Perhaps he meant for you and I to understand that all these qualities—faith, hope, love...and understanding—need to be born again and again within us. And perhaps, that if we will think of the qualities we need most, we will find them within the manger of our hearts, a gift to each of us at our birth—but that we must accept them just as the Babe accepted all the gifts at the manger in the days of Herod.

"An ever lingering perfume of remembrance remains vivid in your consciousness. You have participated in a new birth. A babe's...and your own."

Visit the Manger

Let us imagine that at this very minute you are dreaming a dream—a dream of long ago. In the Hebrew calendar the year is 3749. In your dream you're an official census taker and tax collector, dispatched to Bethlehem to count the people of the lineage of David in order that they might pay their tax tribute.

Your dream finds you walking southward on the hot, dusty roadway from Jerusalem to Bethlehem. You fall in step with another traveler and the two of you engage in conversation which finally turns to the subject of the youth of the day.

"How terrible young people are nowadays," says your new companion.

"Indeed," you agree. "Why only two days ago a group of rowdies stole my donkeys and I'm forced to *walk* on this journey to Bethlehem. It will cost me all I earn to replace them."

"Hoodlums—nothing but hoodlums," says your companion. "They may have been the same scoundrels that defaced the walls of my home with vile and vulgar markings. I'd like to see them chained to oars in the Roman galleons."

Near the top of a small rise in the road, the two of you pause to rest, seating yourselves on a large flat rock. After a moment you notice two obviously weary travelers also heading south toward Bethlehem. An older man is leading a donkey upon which a young woman is riding. They, too, pause to rest a little distance away. The young woman dismounts. She is obviously with child. The man lays a covering on the ground for her to rest upon.

A little boy, who has been following them, engages the man in conversation. After a moment he takes the donkey's halter, leads the animal to a nearby well and gives it a handful of grass and some water. He then returns the animal to its owner. The young woman mounts again and they continue their journey.

You wonder about what you've witnessed. How different were the young boy's acts from the image of youth you so recently had been discussing. "Probably," you think to yourself, "he's an exception—one in a thousand."

As your dream carries you onward you reflect upon the changing customs of the time. "It seems," you remark, "that women, specially the younger ones, no longer want to work as they once did. Gathering food and fuel, caring for children, cooking and cleaning house, spinning flax, making galabeyas, caring for livestock—that's all they have to do. Yet they complain, and sometimes they even try to discuss religious and political matters though they very well know only men are intelligent enough to understand such matters!"

Even as these unseemly thoughts wander through your mind you pass by a small house from which comes the angry sound of a man's voice berating a protesting young girl (probably his daughter) for her lack of attention to her responsibilities as a member of his household—she, according to the custom of the time, being his property.

Your fellow traveler has a comment. "The world," he says, "is going to the dogs. Look at the commercialism, the sellers of souvenirs around the Temple. The bazaars are filled with thieves who will snatch your money pouch and disappear before you know it."

"In this world," you conclude, "there's nothing but misery, thievery and disappointment."

Finally you arrive in Bethlehem and begin your official duties...counting, counting, collecting the tax tribute from each person. One day you hear nothing but excited conversation about three noble and obviously wealthy visitors. They've just arrived and have gone to the cattle stall behind the inn where a baby was recently born. Some speculate they might even be kings.

"Aha," you think, "I see the possibility of a royal profit in this fortunate situation." You have pleasant visions of collecting an enormous tax from them, for they must truly be wealthy if they are kings, so you hurry to the described place.

An amazing scene surrounds you. As you step within the enclosed area, you are drawn into a hushed atmosphere that seems mystically charged with a special energy. To your surprise, you recognize the older man and young woman you had previously seen while resting on your journey. The woman had evidently given birth to her child, for there was a babe in a makeshift crib in the manger. The three noblemen are there too. But there is no clamor to win their attention and perhaps their favor. Even *they* seem entranced by the babe in the manger. As you watch intently, each places a gift at the side of the crib. The tiny figure seems strangely alert and consciously aware of everyone's presence.

From time to time, others in the assembled group approach the babe. Among them, you're surprised to see the little boy who fed and watered the donkey, and the young girl who was the subject of her father's wrath. Each person stands silently for a moment in obvious reverence, then moves on. Some leave a trinket. *All*, so it suddenly seems to you, leave in the manger a mysterious kind of something, an energy, from the depths of their inner selves.

So moved are you by this remarkable occurrence that you decide—indeed from within you are impelled—to express your new found feelings. This urge prompts you to join the others. All thoughts of counting and taxing, the very reasons you are in this dusty, crowded town, begin to disappear.

They are replaced by strange, new, but very wonderful ideas which you will consider carefully after you've made your personal visitation to the manger and expressed your esteem and reverence for something far greater than a babe in swaddling clothes. You do not yet know it, but another wonder awaits you.

* * * * * * *

> Now for a few moments, put this book aside, and reexperience your dream thus far. In your mind, bring the dream as near to objective reality as you possibly can. Be in touch again with the atmosphere of the lowly but holy manger. For a few moments feel again the inner sensations of wonder and upliftment—then return to the rest of your dream visit to the light filled manger of long ago.

* * * * * * *

The scene of your dream is so compelling that you cannot bring yourself to leave. Counting and taxing are no longer the most important objectives in your life. You return to a seat on the floor to meditate further on the strange happenings you've witnessed. You find yourself seated between the little boy and the young girl seen earlier in your dream. For some reason this pleases you and you have the feeling that by their presence *they* are in some way contributing to the wondrous occasion *you* are encountering.

Now I don't know whether or not you've ever really experienced this—but you begin to have a dream within a dream. You're dreaming and you know it. In your dream you're having another dream. And this is it:

There's a tremendous outpouring of energy from all the unlimited space of the universe. You're in the center of it. It fills your mind nearly to the point of your being overwhelmed by it. You feel you're in the center of an event of cosmic importance—that there is a return of vital life, a new birth, of light and love to all who will accept them. And there's a personal aspect of it that's meant especially for you.

Suddenly, miraculously, you find yourself one in thought with Gaspar, eldest of the three kings. You realize that his gift of gold is the symbol of the *spirit*—both the Divine Spirit and the human spirit—your spirit as a matter of fact.

Then your thought merges with that of Melchior's, the middle-aged king who offered the gift of frankincense—and you understand that it represents the *body* which your spirit inhabits.

Next, your thought is united with Balthazar's, the youngest king—and you know that his gift of sweet smelling myrrh symbolizes the presence of *mind* refreshed, indeed reborn, as the essential intermediary between spirit and body in your life.

However strongly you strive to grasp and hold your inner dream within a dream, it begins to fade. After a few moments your original dream also slowly dissolves—like a fleeting cloud disappears in the sky. But an ever lingering perfume of remembrance remains vivid in your consciousness. You have participated in a new birth. A babe's...and your own. How wonderful!

Thus, your mystical visit to the manger in the year of 3749 draws to a close. It is eternally intertwined with your dream visit to the manger through this story in this very year. Both are now one within you...will forever be so...you know it and are comforted and strengthened by it.

"So if, perchance
there is a time in
your life you seem to
hear bells that are
harmonious,
melodious, and
bring a glow
to your
consciousness...
believe in them."

The Story of the Bells

The history of bells is so ancient as to be completely lost in antiquity. No one knows their origin. It is believed by some that they originated from the shell of a nut or gourd in which the meat had dried and which rattled when shaken. And no one knows the origin of the story which I shall tell you in a moment.

Nearly every kind of substance has been used to create bells. Clay, wood, copper, bronze, gold, silver, iron—and even leather. It is believed they were originally used for the purpose of warding off evil spirits. Bells were rung at funerals to protect the souls of the dead by driving away unfavorable influences. They were sounded to heal the sick. They were used by priests to sanctify their temples and to announce to the Deity that a congregation was present. Through the centuries bells have tolled the agony of defeat and pealed the joy of triumph.

At Christmas, bells sing a special message of love and birth and rebirth of spiritual, miraculous renewal. And *that* is the message of my story...the Story of the Bells.

* * * * * * *

Elidad was the boy's name, and the sounds of bells were to change his life forever. At the age of twelve he was already growing into the stature which his name signified—"loved of God"—loved in a special way which gives remarkable insight into the truth behind the appearances of things.

There was a sadness in his life however. His father was a man of business acumen, but he could not understand his son. He thought Elidad was but a dreamer. His efforts to change the boy became harsher with passing time, and only widened the distance between them.

One day as Elidad played in front of his father's shop—where supplies for outfitting caravans were made and sold—his attention was mysteriously drawn to some late evening travelers. An older man led a donkey upon which a young woman was riding. He sensed there was a reason for his fascination, but he had no explanation for it. At least, not yet.

He was impelled to stop his play and observe the strangers. He followed at a distance as the travelers made their way to the inn, and from there to the nearby stable which served as shelter for a few animals.

To his amazement, a pallet was prepared for the young woman—and in the following few moments the faint light in the stable grew to such brilliance that his eyes were nearly blinded. He turned away to shield them, but it was several minutes before they seemed normal. As he turned back again, the light had dimmed and the spellbinding cry of a newborn babe brought an understanding smile to his face. He knew that something almost unreal, something historic, something absolutely stupendous had occurred—and he knew that somehow he must play a part in it. But what part? And how?

Elidad remembered when his brothers and sisters were born. Neighbors and relatives had brought gifts. And even as he thought about it, he was amazed to see shepherds from the surrounding countryside arriving at the manger. Some of them did seem to be offering gifts—a woven blanket, a sheepskin comforter, cheese, some dried figs. He wondered what *he* could give that would be worthy of the unusual events he'd witnessed. A daring thought thrust itself into his mind. The golden bells!

His father possessed three small golden bells hidden away for safekeeping. He treasured them above all his possessions. He believed them to be the bells from the robe which God instructed Aaron to make and wear with the ephod when he entered the Holy of Holies. "A golden bell and a pomegranate, a golden bell and a pomegranate, on the hem of the robe round about" were the instructions (see Ex 28:34), so that Aaron might be heard entering and leaving the holy place so he "would not die," as it mysteriously states in the scriptures.

Elidad hurried home, made sure his father was busy elsewhere, took the bells from their hiding place and returned to the stable. Timidly, he approached the manger where the young mother was lulling the Baby to sleep.

As she smiled at him, he became bold enough to place the bells beside the Baby in the crib. They seemed to glow with more than their usual luster. The infant stirred, and in doing so brushed against the bells, causing them to sound softly.

Elidad was saturated with both fear and wonder. Fear, because he thought his gift had wakened the Child. Wonder, because the sound of the bells was not a harsh clanging which was their normal sound. Instead, their tones were mellow, blending into a celestial chorus of harmonics that filled the manger and radiated in every direction so that passersby paused in their scurrying and looked about in vain for the source of the delightful sounds that surrounded them from every direction.

Elidad's wonder overcame his fear. He was inspired by the sound, lifted on high as never before in his life. He watched in awe as others entered the stable—some with material gifts and some with gifts of the spirit. Each of them seemed in some way to be rewarded. For some, the signs of weariness and care faded from their faces. In others he perceived a look of joy, and even ecstacy. And some, even sick townspeople he knew, were healed of their illnesses. He was sure that each person received a blessing far beyond any which could be bestowed by anyone he had ever known. In spite of his talent for insight, Elidad had no explanation for the uncommon events he witnessed.

* * * * * * *

> You now have the opportunity to join Elidad at the manger. Leave your own inner gift with the Babe, and for yourself experience the rewards of oneness with the Christ Spirit as it is reborn in you.
>
> Perhaps, on another level of your own being, you too will hear the sound of the bells, and experience the unique result of having their harmonious vibrations mingle with yours.

* * * * * * *

Elidad finally returned home, bursting to tell his parents all he had seen and experienced. His euphoria was destined to be shattered. He found his father in a blistering rage.

"Someone has stolen my bells! My precious bells! My bells from Aaron's robe!" He shouted at Elidad, "Do *you* know what happened to them?"

Elidad was a truthful boy. "Yes, Father, I took the bells and gave them as a gift to a baby just born in the stable near the inn."

Naturally his father was furious. His punishment of Elidad was characteristically immediate and harsh, and the boy's tears were no balm for his aching body, which bore the bruises inflicted by his father. But worst of all was his father's declaration that he would immediately go to the stable and take the bells away from the little one to whom they were given. Elidad's protests fell upon unhearing ears and a mood that was not to be softened.

Late though it was, his father rushed from the house and headed for the stable. He was perhaps fifty paces from his destination, in a particularly shadowed place, when he was attacked by two ruffians. Even strengthened by his rage, he was no match for the robbers and, after a number of painful blows, was overcome and held securely on the ground.

Just as one of the ruffians demanded his money pouch, growing sounds of many bells filled the area. The sounds of a caravan, perhaps fifty camels or more. Caravans did not usually travel that late at night, and from the sound this obviously was a large one.

"Run," hissed one of the robbers—and they both speedily vanished into the darkness.

Elidad's father took several moments to regain his composure. As he slowly rose from the ground he looked about for the caravan. There was none in sight! For that matter, there was no further sound of bells either, though he'd heard them clearly, as did the ruffians.

He took several more steps toward the stable where the brilliance of a strange light was slowly diminishing. Enough of it remained for him to see that all inside were sleeping—all, that is, except the Babe. There was a slight movement in the Child's body. His arm raised ever so little, but enough to see that clasped in the tiny fingers was the strand of precious bells. They sounded softly, as though with a special message for Elidad's father.

As he looked at them, and listened to them, his hurts vanished, his anger subsided, his heart melted, and it seemed to him that the bells had come into their rightful ownership. He turned away, hardly believing the amazing change in himself which had occurred in the Child's presence. He walked slowly home, each step increasing his determination to mend his relationship with his son.

The years passed. Elidad, reaching early manhood, struck out on his own and opened a small shop near Caesarea in the north country on the coast. He made and mended harness for the caravans and became known as the best harnessmaker in the entire region. Near the close of one day, at the dim rear of his shop among the leather straps and thongs and metal buckles and other supplies, he noticed a small bell, rusty with age.

As he touched it, though it wasn't gold, it reminded him once more of the scenes he had witnessed in his memory hundreds of times...the little family in the stable, the golden bells, the wondrous light, the gifts given and received—especially the gift of his father's love.

Suddenly he thought he actually heard the mellow sound again. So strong and clear it seemed that he went to the front of the shop to see if another miracle was happening. Hardly anyone was in sight. No one but an older man, a woman, and a child, weary and dusty from an obviously lengthy journey.

"They look as though they must have walked from as far away as Egypt," he thought.

He continued to watch as they passed the shop and walked on along the road. For a moment he thought there was a muted glowing light around the boy, but he dismissed it as a trick of the sinking sunlight.

"Strange," he mused. "The road they're taking leads but to Nazareth...and who in the world would want to go there!"

* * * * * * *

So if, perchance, there is a time in your life you seem to hear bells that are harmonious, melodious, and bring a glow to your consciousness...believe in them. They may be the very same bells I've told you about in this story, still ringing their message of love down through the ages.

"There was a vague stirring, a kind of reverie, in his mind. He seemed to travel through space while yet remaining on the hillside."

The Shepherd Who Disbelieved

It was a few nights after the full moon. Two young shepherds, Hoshea and Gershon, were talking idly while their flocks became calm for the night. The air hushed. The evening breeze stilled. Moon and stars were bright, but silent, against the blue-black velvet backdrop of the sky. Even the crackle of their tiny fire seemed muted.

"What do you think," asked Hoshea, "of the talk about this great leader who's supposed to be coming?"

Gershon stared at his friend in amazement. "Surely you don't believe in that nonsense!" he exclaimed. "Why that old story has been going around for at least five hundred years." His disgust at the thought was obvious.

"But this time," Hoshea responded, "the stories are told by responsible people. Even Iscah's father believes them."

Iscah was the daughter of the man who owned the flocks which the young men guarded. She was as beautiful as a grazing fawn, graceful as a doe. Bright as the evening star on a moonless night. Both young men loved her dearly. Her father was considered the wisest man in the community. If he believed in the coming of a great leader, it became a matter of great weight in the minds of others.

But Gershon had a mind of his own. He didn't readily accept, nor was he easily moved by, beliefs which were commonly held. He thought the idea of someone being born for the specific purpose of political leadership was illogical foolishness, and he didn't hesitate to express his opinion.

"Hoshea," he said, "when will you come to your senses and stop believing the prattle of those who yearn so strongly they make fiction seem like truth! No matter how much you believe, nothing ever happens."

"The problem with you, Gershon, is that you've had so many troubles you now don't believe anything. You have to believe in *something*."

"No. I don't believe *any* of those miracle stories. You have to take total leave of your senses to think that any of the miracles which our forefathers tell about ever really happened. And as for a Messiah, well—!"

The young friends fell silent, each reinforcing his own opinion with additional unspoken thoughts. Time passed, possibly an hour, without further conversation.

The night quiet was abruptly broken by the sound of someone running toward them. Then a shout. "Hoshea—Gershon—!" It was Iscah's voice. As she approached, breathless, agitated, she said, "You must come with me. We've seen and heard the most amazing things. There was a star in the heavens. There were angelic voices. We were told to go to the village. The one we've been waiting for has arrived. The prophecy is fulfilled! Come, we must hurry and catch up with the others." She stopped only for want of breath.

Hoshea immediately caught and reflected her excitement. "Wonderful. Let's go at once!" He started off with Iscah, but stopped when he realized Gershon wasn't following.

"Come on Gershon," he urged. "We must hurry!"

"Hurry?" Gershon questioned. "After five hundred years we have to run off in the middle of the night because of a star and a supposed angel speaking some kind of foolishness? And in Bethlehem?"

"Please Gershon," Iscah pleaded.

"No!" Gershon was stubborn. "I don't believe in such rubbish. You two go if you wish—I'll stay with the sheep. Then tomorrow, when you've come back to your right minds, I'll talk some sense to you."

The moment had no urgency whatever for Gershon, but for Iscah and Hoshea it was irresistibly compelling. They hurried off and soon merged into the dark. In a few moments their excited chattering and the rapid crunch of their footsteps died away. Gershon was left alone in stillness and darkness.

For a brief time it did seem to him that one of the many stars overhead shone slightly brighter than the others. But it quickly dimmed as the bitter frustrations of the years surged to a stormy turmoil in his consciousness. Especially galling were the disillusions he'd suffered. Broken promises and unfulfilled expectations had solidified a pattern of disbelief in his mind, and chilled the warmth that a young heart should experience.

As Gershon wrestled with his loneliness, he was distracted by an unexpected sound. It was as though a conch shell horn had sounded somewhere, and this was its distant echo, reflecting off the faraway heavens. It seemed to be almost a fanfare, such as played for important personages on those seldom occasions when they came to the village. The wonder of it all was so powerful that he thought for a time he was losing consciousness.

The tones didn't really fade away, they just seemed to be withdrawn into the heights above him. And he was startled to hear them replaced by a voice which said, "You have heard the trumpet of battle, the call to arms in the human struggle for power and riches. It was played by the spirit of conflict—the spirit of contention—nation against nation, man against his brother, husband against wife, children against their parents. In another age that sound will gradually dim, and finally become silent."

For a long time Gershon was shaken and speechless with wonder. Then he heard the tinkling of faraway camel bells. There were three distinct tones, indicating three camels and riders, passing by, invisible in the darkness.

"Odd," he thought. "In the middle of the night they, too, are headed in the direction of Bethlehem."

He didn't really fall asleep. His mind was too busy contemplating his unusual experience. Yet he wasn't conscious of passing time either. There was a vague stirring, a kind of reverie, in his mind. He seemed to travel through space while yet remaining on the hillside. He glided over gently rolling hills where unattended flocks stood motionless and apparently unafraid. He drifted to the center of the village where he saw three obviously great personages enter a stable and gaze with awe and reverence upon a baby in a manger. He even saw his friends, Iscah and Hoshea, do the same. And he saw something else, something so profound that it transcended the centuries. Something so strange that it taxed his mind even to try to comprehend.

* * * * * * *

I'll tell you what he witnessed on that incredible night after we meditatively join the Wise Men at the manger—

For a few moments, relax as completely as possible. Visualize yourself resting at night on a hillside near Bethlehem. Your attention is drawn to a brilliant star that seems to be shining just for you. You know that its rays have a message for you, so you relax still further and mentally express the idea that you are receptive and ready for it. The message bids you to visit the manger.

You walk down the winding hillside path, past an olive grove, through the narrow streets to the place where the Babe lies in the manger. You join the Wise Men and others in the special kind of silence in which thoughts and feelings are expressed without the need for words.

Quiet joy, peace, oneness, love—these are the feelings you experience. You have the odd sensation of being humbled and exalted at the same time. And you know you are included in a Great Presence. Slowly the scene fades from your vision and you are ready to continue the story as though you are part of a new world, a higher world, a better world.

* * * * * * *

What was the vision that transcended the centuries? The mystical scene which unfolded before Gershon disclosed a view of the future, something he could not possibly understand. Mingling with the Wise Men and the shepherds was a strangely dressed people, speaking an unknown tongue. He saw you and me there too!

How long his mystical midnight reverie continued he never knew. But he remembered that at one point he again heard the trumpet sound. Celestial it seemed. Tones of peace. The melody of love. Notes tumbled together, yet floated harmoniously on the soft breeze.

And as they ebbed into silence, again the voice. "You have heard the trumpet of peace. *It* was sounded by the spirit of love. After the struggles and the birthing labor pains of the ages, *it* is the melody that one day will be the song and the symphony of all humankind." The voice fell silent.

Slivers of dawn began to appear over the nearby hills. And with them came Iscah and Hoshea. Bubbling with excitement they recounted all they had seen and heard in the stable during the mysterious night before. To their amazement, Gershon listened quietly and made no protest that their statements were gibberish, as he had previously.

However, he didn't tell them of *his* experience. He really wanted to share it, yet it seemed so personal a treasure that he could not.

He could only say, "Wonderful, mysterious, and unexplainable things happen, even in the lives of those who don't believe."

But to himself he commented, "And a new world began in a stable just last night."

I was there—and you were there. He was thinking of Iscah and Hoshea. He was also thinking of you and me.

"It was an
eternal star....
Its light shines
by day as well as
night, and the
one who sees it
is never alone."

Did You See the Star?

Moza, a noted Arab astronomer living in the northern city of Gadara, began his journey to Jerusalem in a very bad mood. He had already been robbed of his money pouch and half the funds he'd saved for his journey.

The unfortunate incident contributed heavily to his distaste for what he considered an unpleasant but necessary task. Like most of us, he would rather not do what he considered he had to do. Under the best of circumstances I would not describe Moza as the most pleasant or considerate person in the world. And his usual distasteful mood had deteriorated.

He knew that, among the astronomers of the land, there was excitement and controversy about a new star. "How ridiculous," he told a group of fellow astronomers. "I'll investigate for myself and settle the matter once and for all."

By Moza's calculations there was indeed an alignment of three heavenly bodies which, due to the resulting brightness in the heavens, could be interpreted by the unknowing and the unreasonable as a new star in the night sky. But actually a new star? An impossibility!

Quite egotistically, Moza reasoned that it was *his* responsibility to educate the unenlightened among his peers, and the masses, about what he considered a potential truth-damaging misconception. And he reasoned that the only way to do this was to visit the area that seemed to be the center of the controversy—Jerusalem.

In spite of the loss of his money, he considered his mission important enough to proceed with his journey. So he saddled his camel, a gaunt beast with a personality somewhat similar to his master's.

The first morning passed uneventfully. There were few travelers, and he avoided them, for he was a solitary man—and besides, he felt none of them equaled his level of intelligence. "Why should I bother with them?" he often asked.

As he rode along a hardly visible trail winding through a pass in the low mountains, three men on horses suddenly appeared, apparently from behind one of the foothills. Moza immediately recognized them as Sicarii, members of a noted band of robbers and assassins. As they came abreast of him they brandished their knives, grasped the reins of his camel, and shouted for him to dismount. He did so, readily. In a brief moment the thieves stripped him of his food, camel, saddle and all his supplies except the remainder of his money, about a dozen denarii, which he had thoughtfully hidden in the folds of his robe at the beginning of his journey.

Thus was Moza left alone in a strange country, wondering what misfortune might next befall him. He found a small deserted granary in which he shivered sleeplessly through the night, for now he had only his robe to protect himself from the penetrating cold night air. He was up with the sun, hoping to arrive soon at the next village where he might purchase a little food and a blanket for the rest of the journey.

He hadn't enough silver denarii to purchase another camel, so he was resigned to the long exhausting walk. But he had been informed that others of his profession would be in Jerusalem and he believed that, because of his reputation, they would undoubtedly assist him.

"And then," he thought, "I will open their eyes to the foolishness of their expectations about a fanciful new star portending some dreamed up event of great magnitude."

The next day, about midmorning, Moza heard the rapid clomping of hooves behind him on the trail. The sounds must have come from a large group for a great dust cloud accompanied them. Hardly had he made this observation than they were reining in their camels at his side. Moza was astonished that there were but three camel riders, obviously foreigners, and two pack donkeys in the group. Camels and donkeys seemed eager for a few moments rest, but the three men seemed quite impatient.

They were friendly enough, however, greeting Moza in his own language. Their bearing hinted at nobility, or perhaps even royalty. They were obviously learned.

One of them explained, "We are priests and astronomers. A brilliant star has illumined the approach of a unique event in the history of humankind, and we are following it to the important place the star will soon designate by coming to rest. That place, we have just been told, is the village of Bethlehem." Then, he concluded with a question, "Did *you* see the star?"

Moza was astounded that such educated men should be so stupid. He answered with a scornful question of his own. "Are *you* also looking for that fantasy? You seem too intelligent to engage in such a worthless enterprise." His tone of voice portrayed his usual surly animosity toward anyone whose views did not coincide with his.

"No!" He was shouting now, his voice rising in anger. "And I *won't* see a star because there *is* no star!"

Apparently untroubled by Moza's rudeness, the three men thanked him courteously and rode rapidly away. We know who they were and where they were headed, so with the magic of imagination let us go quickly to the manger and see for ourselves what the Wise Men will discover when *they* arrive.

* * * * * * *

Will you please take part in this story? You have the imagination and ability to do so. Simply be quiet for a few moments. Direct your thoughts to flow back to the time and place of the Birth.

There you see the Babe, Mary and Joseph, the shepherds and others. And now the three Wise Men arrive. You feel an exhilarating change in an atmosphere already charged with the electricity of expectancy. Each of the royal visitors in turn approaches the Babe and leaves a symbolic gift.

In your mind, and through your heart, you do the same. You leave the gift of your own presence in tribute to the Great Presence. And you sense a responsive surge of energy filling your being.

Afterward, the focus of your consciousness returns to here and now, and you continue the story and journey of Moza, the disappointed astronomer.

* * * * * * *

Several days later, Moza followed the trail of the star seekers until he, too, arrived in Bethlehem. Not once had he been able to see the star which so many others described to him, and he saw no evidence of it now. The village, in fact, was engulfed in early evening darkness, and seemed deserted.

There was a lone light at the inn, and at his inquiry the innkeeper told him there might be someone at the stable who could give him information about the star. "For myself," the innkeeper said, "I don't believe in any special star, but I *will* say there were strange goings on around here for several days."

With a feeble candle provided by the innkeeper, Moza found the stable. As he entered his heart suddenly pounded with the feeling that the stable was filled with invisible forces. He reminded himself he didn't believe in such things, but he felt them nevertheless, and the feeling wouldn't go away. Suddenly, at the outer edge of the flickering light cast by his candle, he was aware of a small boy, watching him intently.

Slowly, the boy spoke. "Did you see the star?" he asked. His tone was so imploring, so filled with hope, that Moza's usual gruff demeanor melted like a spring snow in a mountain stream.

"No," he said, as if apologizing for not having had the very experience he so frequently derided.

"That's too bad," said the boy. "Neither did I. My mother did, and she came here with my older brothers and sisters. They all saw the star, and the Baby, the three foreigners, and all the others. They're all gone now.

"I had to stay home and tend the flock in the hills. My father was sick and had to stay home too. My mother said she prayed and asked for him to be well, and when they got home he no longer had any pain in his stomach.

"But,"—the boy's voice became melancholy—"I was left out of everything. I didn't get to see anything, or hear anything, like the other shepherds did." The disappointed youngster became silent, and finally fell sound asleep.

The candle flickered out, and Moza sat quietly in the darkness. The many disappointments of *his* life began to flow through his consciousness in an agonizing stream. Finally, overtaken by exhaustion, he too drifted into sleep.

It was nearly morning when dream visions began appearing to him, as they often do for all of us. In the visions he heard excited voices filtering out of the stillness. He was dreaming, he knew, yet oddly at the same time he seemed awake. He again became conscious of the energy filling the manger and he knew it lingered there from events of the past few days.

He saw people (you and me perhaps), shepherds, the Wise Men, children, mothers and fathers, business people, homemakers, tax collectors, the poor, the pain ridden and the troubled. And he saw a wondrous glow radiate from the crib into the life of each person present, including the little boy, and even into himself. All eyes focussed on the Babe in the crib.

He was suddenly awakened from this remarkable reverie by the boy's voice. "Did you see the star?" was again his plaintive question.

Moza thought carefully before answering. He spoke slowly, with words that came from a newly warmed heart rather than a cold, calculating mind.

"Yes," he said. "I saw the star. It wasn't a star in the heavens which might appear for a time then no longer be seen."

"What kind of star was it?"—the boy's voice was troubled, for he thought he'd been left out again.

"It was an eternal star," said Moza. "Its light shines by day as well as night, and the one who sees it is never alone.

It's an inner star that gives each person the great gift of understanding. It's like being born again as a new person. But you don't look for it in the sky—you look inside yourself."

Both the boy and the man fell silent for a time. Finally, hesitantly, the youngster said, "I think *I* see the star too."

"I'm sure you do," Moza replied. Then he smiled as he realized that for the first time in his life he was accepting the opinion of another person—and a child at that.

Though strangers, an instant bond was forged between boy and man, a kind of cosmic companionship—two persons separated by age and education, found oneness through experience and belief. After a moment, Moza took the boy's hand in his own, and together they walked from the stable's dim light into the dawn of a new day.

"It was a breathless, electric moment for everyone. More than that it was a moment that seemed to transend time and space and caught them all up in a fusion of love and joy and fulfillment."

An Angel Named George

Once upon a time, but not too long ago, a young man named Chris had a very unusual experience. Though he was but fifteen years old, he'd already met more of life's challenges than many of us.

Chris was a victim of Down's Syndrome. That may have been part of the reason for his most unusual imagination. Even his family, and his very few friends, said they were often startled by his strange stories. "He imagines more strange things than anyone I ever knew," they would say.

The reason they said this, and his mother and father said it more often than anyone, is because Chris was always telling about a friend no one else ever saw! From the time when he was only ten or eleven, he would describe visits and conversations with this unseen friend—unseen, that is, to everyone but Chris.

No one believed that what Chris described was actually happening. They attributed it to his congenital condition. Family or friends would listen to his strange stories and try to convince him he was seeing someone who wasn't really there. And you know how it is sometimes, when people are different, who knows where their ideas come from?

"His name is George," Chris would insist. "He's a little smaller than I am, and a little younger. He has dark hair and a big smile. He sometimes comes to see me in the afternoon, but not very often. Mostly he comes at night when I'm asleep, and he takes me places. He must be an angel."

"Where does he take you?" asked Chris's mother, Ellen.

"To the park," answered Chris. "And sometimes in the afternoon to the ball game or the zoo."

You really cannot blame anyone for thinking Chris was only using his imagination. They say Down's Syndrome children do create worlds of their own, where they can find a broader acceptance. Everyone just knew this had to be true for Chris.

So his mother would merely smile gently at his stories. She made allowance for his differences and she really believed she was simply dealing with childhood fantasies that would soon be outgrown. In fact, she vaguely remembered her husband's mother telling of *her* having similar experiences when *she* was a little girl.

Not able to have additional children of their own, Ellen and her husband had applied to an adoption agency for another child. They felt they would be a happier and more complete family with two boys. However, several months had passed without their wish being fulfilled. This was a disappointment for they wanted to find their family addition before Christmas, which was only a few days away.

"If we ever hear from the adoption service," she said to Chris's father, Dave, "perhaps one day we'll have another youngster for him to play with and he'll forget these fantasies. Sometimes I wonder if they'll ever call."

His father, however, was neither as patient nor as tolerant of his son's unusual accounts of an angel named George. "Listen Chris," he'd say, "you're having some kind of crazy dream. There's not anything *real* about it. It doesn't happen. It's just your imagination." Then he would try to explain how imagination worked, but Chris couldn't understand it.

Chris's mother told his father he shouldn't talk that way. "You know," she said, "Chris is often lonely and unhappy and he's just trying to make up for it. He's different from the other kids." But she couldn't change his father's mind.

One morning Chris announced that George had taken him to a place where there were lots of children. "They all looked sad," he said, "and when they talked they wished they could have a happy Christmas like other boys and girls.

"Some of them knew George," he said. "And George had me tell them how much fun Christmas can be. But most of them wouldn't believe it."

Another time, Chris told his mother that George had taken him to Grandma's house during the night, and that George and Grandma talked for a long time. "George told her he needed help," said Chris, "and Grandma promised she would do all she could to help him."

"What did Grandma look like?" Ellen asked. Chris described her dark hair, her glasses, her red apron with a white bow on each shoulder.

After listening to the story, Chris's mother took a deep breath and was quiet for a long time. "Don't tell your father about this," she said finally, and she had a good reason which she preferred to keep quiet about.

"The 'Grandma' in Chris's fantasy," she thought to herself, "could be no one but my husband's mother...and she died when Chris was only a baby. But how could the child have described her so well—especially the red apron with the white bows?" She remembered that Grandma had worn that very apron every Christmas for years. She knew her husband would be terribly upset at what he would call another fantasy, even more than before because it involved his deceased mother.

Then, Christmas morning arrived. The family gathered around the tree in the living room to open gifts. It was then that Chris told his parents the strangest story of all.

"Last night," he said, "George took me on a time trip!"

"What in the world is a time trip?" His father's words dripped with sarcastic skepticism.

But his father's obvious disbelief didn't dampen Chris's excitement. Nor did he hesitate to explain. "We went back in time. Grandma was with us!"

Chris's mother caught her breath apprehensively. She looked at her husband whose eyes were wide in shock and disbelief. He was about to speak but she motioned him to remain silent.

Chris continued his strange story. "We went back to what Grandma said was the first Christmas. There were lots of neat animals around in this stable. George and I wanted to pet them, but Grandma told us to go inside. She told us who the people were. And that all of us were there to welcome this new baby to earth.

"Everything was quiet for a long time. Different people came in to look at the Baby and leave gifts. One man came in on crutches. Grandma said he was praying. When he left he put his crutches down and walked out. A woman came in crying. When she left she was smiling. I don't know what was happening, but Grandma said they were miracles. George and Grandma and I all prayed with everyone else."

"What did *you* pray for?" asked Chris's mother.

"I prayed that you would get to see George."

After a long silent pause, Chris continued. "Then three men dressed in robes came in. They touched each of us on the forehead, and the Baby too, and said they would help us with our problems."

* * * * * * *

Before continuing the story, pause a moment for your own meditative visit to the manger. Let your own imaginative faculty guide you to time past. Visit with shepherds, townspeople, even the holy family.

You'll probably discover that their problems then were very similar to yours today. If you wish, visualize Chris, George and Grandma there, too. You may wish to join them and try to hear what George and Grandma are praying about. When you've finished your imaginative reverie, return to our story and its unusual ending.

* * * * * * *

Chris continued his strange story of a trip through time and space with Grandma and George.

"Lots of others came," he said. "And every once in a while Grandma would whisper, 'Another miracle.' Finally she said we'd have to leave. But before we did she took George's hand and they went up to the Baby. I couldn't hear too well, but I think she asked the Baby to do something for George."

He paused a moment, then asked, "How could that baby help George?"

Before there was time for Chris's father to make one of his usual sarcastic comments, the doorbell rang. Obviously disturbed at the interruption, he nevertheless went to answer it. In a moment he was back in the living room, looking like you might expect someone to look who has just seen a ghost.

"Ellen, and Chris..." he hesitated, struggling to control himself. "The people from the adoption service are here. They want us to meet someone they believe we might like to have join our family..." He could speak no further. He simply stood aside as a young boy came through the doorway. The boy was just a little smaller, and just a little younger, than Chris, *with dark hair—and a big smile.*

It was a breathless, electric moment for everyone. More than that, it was a moment that seemed to transcend time and space and caught them all up in a fusion of love and joy and fulfillment.

Chris glanced at the boy no longer than a fraction of a second.

"George!" he shouted, and the boy moved swiftly to clasp Chris's hand as would two great and dear friends, meeting after a long separation!

Now I ask you something. Do you believe it was the same George who befriended Chris in his "fantasies"? Had he been at the orphanage, waiting for someone to fill *his* Christmas wish and his whole life with love? Was he the one who had appealed to Grandma, and with her to the Christed Babe, for help?

Well, I'll tell you this...if you really want to enjoy Christmas, if you really want to discover the Christ Spirit that is born in you at this momentous and glorious time of year, you'll believe...you'll believe...yes, you'll *have* to believe.

"...he realized it was time for him to go on into the celestial mansions of life. He pondered long upon the adventure ahead. He knew no fear, nor had he ever since that eventful day at the manger."

The Mystery of the Gentle Heart

A shepherd, Jaroah by name, tended his flock in a little valley not far from Bethlehem. It was a beautiful valley but, like so many places of seeming serenity, hidden dangers lurked in wait for the unwary. On either side steep cliffs provided hiding places for the mountain lions that, from time to time, raided the flocks of sheep in order to feed their own hungry families.

Now Jaroah was a good shepherd who cared for his flock with both tenderness and bravery. He prospered. His flock increased and became the largest in the area. He was proud of his success. It meant that soon he would have accumulated a dowry large enough to petition for the privilege of being wed to Vashti, whom he long had loved. Finally they were indeed betrothed and they looked forward eagerly to the day of their wedding.

But one night an especially ferocious and hungry mountain lion crept into the center of the flock and seized a lamb. As the intruder was carrying off his prize, Jaroah intercepted him and attempted to beat him off with his shepherd's staff.

The wily cat, however, was an accomplished, veteran fighter. Time after time he rushed the shepherd, dodged his blows and with powerful claws ripped his tunic and inflicted horribly deep gashes on his arms, chest and face. Jaroah fought furiously and imposed his own punishment on the lion. It finally could withstand his blows no longer and scurried off into the darkness.

Jaroah, weak from his long struggle and loss of blood, dropped to the ground, exhausted, and slept the rest of the night. In the morning he made his way to the home of Vashti and her parents for help. Vashti's brother went to the valley to guard the flock, and Vashti became Jaroah's nurse.

Infection had already set in his wounds, and even though Vashti skillfully applied ointments and healing balms, it was really too late to prevent highly visible, unsightly scars which remained after the days had passed and he regained his strength.

Finally, he was again able to return to his shepherd's duties, and the weeks passed uneventfully. The size of his flock continued to increase as he cared for it skillfully. But another catastrophe befell him.

Although his eyes and ears were keen, and normally he would become aware of the slightest hint of approaching danger, nevertheless he was surprised by a trio of robbers. Before he realized it, they leaped upon him and beat him unmercifully. Again he fought with all the valor and strength he possessed, but he was no match for the three ruffians. So fierce and unmerciful was their attack that Jaroah's right leg was broken. They left him for dead and stole his prized flock of sheep, leaving him penniless.

The next morning he was discovered by Vashti's father, who took him to his home, where again Vashti nursed him back to health. However, his leg was now so crippled that it was difficult for him to walk, and even then he limped badly. At this point a still further blow befell him.

Vashti's parents observed that he was no longer handsome and was really too crippled to care for sheep. Because he had lost his entire flock, and was now destitute, they annulled the betrothal agreement and, with it, Jaroah's heart.

With the loss of his love, the last light disappeared from his life. He now had nothing worthwhile to live for; he lacked the heart to discipline himself to work in any useful endeavor. His mind became bitter as his heart was hardened. He struggled to maintain life by wandering to distant places, begging from house to house—a complete and worthless derelict.

Had he remained near his home, perhaps in the company of other nearby shepherds, he might have seen the star and heard the angelic voices that proclaimed the Great Incarnation about to occur. But this privilege, too, he was denied.

As he went from door to door, begging a crust, or even a few crumbs of bread, his heart's only wish was that he might somehow get out of the world with all its woes. His many travels finally took him again near Bethlehem. From having visited the village when he was a boy, he remembered there was an inn, and a stable nearby. He knew better than to seek admittance to the inn, for his appearance was disreputable, his clothing in rags, and his scarred face enough to repulse even the most compassionate of innkeepers. He had absolutely no money with which to purchase either food or lodging, but he thought he might find a place to sleep for a night or two in the stable.

Remaining in the shadows, he avoided the groups of people passing him from time to time, most of then grumbling about having to pay the head tax required of them. He circled behind the inn and found the stable he remembered from his youth.

He entered and went to the stall furthest from the entrance where darkness was deepest and where he felt he could hide, yet have a little warmth and comfort during the night. He had no sooner made a pitiful straw pallet for himself than he became aware that others were entering the stall adjacent to his. He saw them to be a man and a woman. She was obviously with child.

An atmosphere of excitement pervaded the stable. Even the animals, whose warmth of body took a little sharpness off the crisp night, behaved in a very strange manner. Even so, distraught and terribly exhausted from all his ordeals, Jaroah lay down and was soon sound asleep.

He didn't know how much later it occurred, but he was suddenly awakened by the cry of a baby. Slowly and painfully, he rose from his pallet and peered through a crack into the adjacent stall. He watched in amazement as a newborn child was wrapped in swaddling clothes and laid in a crib. The reason for his astonishment was the light that seemed to shine around the tiny form. The Babe was silent now, yet a sense of exhilaration filled the atmosphere.

As he continued to watch, he was puzzled to observe that others were entering the stable, approaching the tiny form in the crib and kneeling in obvious reverence. He could not overhear much that was spoken, yet it seemed to him that he could catch, now and then, a phrase of adoration. He was perplexed. Why should anyone treat a newborn child, just arriving, and in a stable, with such respect and awe? It was beyond his comprehension, but the constantly changing scene before him kept him glued to the crack in the stall, and he continued to watch in total amazement.

To add to his bewilderment, he observed that those who visited the Baby were not all peasants and shepherds. Some of them, it was plain to see, were persons of repute and substance. Then his wonderment was compounded ten-fold when he saw three stately men arrive at the manger. Obviously, they were of noble birth and had traveled a great distance. They placed gifts at the crib and he watched the tiny hand of the Babe raise, as if in recognition. He noted the reaction of each of these three, reactions which indicated they had *received* more than they had given, although he saw nothing of substance being given to them.

The scene constantly changed. It seemed to Jaroah that a multitude of people knelt before the Child. Many arrived with looks of pain on their faces. They left with countenances obviously radiating joy. It was far too much to comprehend. Finally, he again laid on his pallet and fell into slumber, exhausted in mind and body.

* * * * * * *

> While the procession of visitors has momentarily ceased, take a few moments to use your own powers of imagery in a quiet visit to the manger. Gently, with no straining, direct your inner self to make the journey to the Birthplace. In your meditative mode, use your inner feeling sense to detect an interchange of energy with the always new-birthing Christ Spirit. When you've completed your meditation, return to the story of the gentle heart.

* * * * * * *

When Jaroah awoke it was evening and all was quiet in the manger. He peered again into the adjoining stall and saw the family was still there, but no other persons were present. After considering the events he had witnessed, he overcame his timidity and his concern that his repulsive appearance would frighten the family and decided that he, too, would kneel before the Babe.

Neither the man nor the woman seemed concerned at his presence, and Jaroah wondered if they hadn't known of it all the time. They only smiled upon him and nodded as if in recognition, although he couldn't remember ever having known them. As he knelt before the manger, he saw the many gifts others had left, and desperately wished that he, too, might leave something for this new life. His consternation at his problems, losing his love and worldly possessions had, been so overpowering that he left home with only one possession to his name. It was a small talisman, a piece of wood, upon which was carved but one word, "Love."

It had been given to him by his mother when he was but a boy, and he had carried it faithfully through the years to this very solemn moment. It was his only and therefore his dearest possession. He drew it from the little pouch in which he had carried it under his galabeya. He looked at it a moment. It was shiny and smooth from having been often and reverently caressed through the years. Tenderly he placed it on the crib itself. The little Babe dropped his hand on it, fondled it, and smiled.

At that moment it was as though the very breath was drawn from Jaroah's body. He felt a stirring of strange energies within himself, more potent by far than any he had ever felt during the time of his greatest strength and vigor. There was a tensing here and a relaxing there. There was a tingling over the entire surface of his body, as the flesh which had been blighted and scarred was miraculously being renewed.

He put his hand to his right cheek where the deepest wound had been inflicted by the mountain lion, and no longer felt the ugly ridge of the scar that had been there. He touched the leg that had been broken. The bones themselves crackled with a potency which he could not understand. He felt his leg straighten and become as sound as the other. And throughout his whole being he felt an incredible flow of peacefulness and inner harmony, and with it a returning strength and vitality.

He looked at himself in amazement, and then noticed that the man in the stall was offering him a new galabeya and a shepherd's staff. He was so overcome he could only mumble his appreciation. He hurried back to his own stall, changed clothes and immediately set out upon the roadway to return to his former home.

A ewe and four or five lambs that evidently strayed from some unobservant shepherd's flock attached themselves to him, and followed after him.

He came again to the familiar valley where he had spent so many happy years. Suddenly he was alerted once more by that old familiar, frightening sound—the growl of a mountain lion. Investigation showed that a mother lion had been wounded, and lay near death with her hungry cubs lying at her side. Even in her weakened condition she was trying to obtain food for them, but she could not even rise. Jaroah was tempted to club them all to death. But he remembered the talisman he had so recently placed in the crib—and he remembered its inscription—LOVE. He obtained some milk from the ewe, put it into the shallow depressions of a few wayside stones, fed the cubs, and went upon his way.

A little further along, he was apprehended by robbers who demanded money from him, but of course he had none. Again he remembered the talisman and said, "I do have a gift to give you," and he began to tell the story of his healing, really the only great gift he could pass on to others.

He spoke with such utter sincerity and simplicity that they listened intently, were compelled to believe him, and finally asked how they too might find the manger.

Jaroah returned to his former home, wed Vashti, and spent many years in happiness and prosperity. As old age came to him, and his sons had taken over his duties as caretaker of the flocks, he realized that it was time for him to go on into the celestial mansions of life. He pondered long upon the adventure that was ahead of him. He knew no fear, nor had he ever since that eventful day at the manger.

In his mind he visualized the tiny Babe one more time. A shining realization flooded his consciousness, and he understood the reason for his own recovery from physical defects and his success in family and business life. Again, he lived through the scene. He recalled that as he placed the little talisman in the crib, the Babe had grasped it and smiled, and in so doing had given *him* a gift in return. In the closing moments of his life, he realized for the first time what it really was, a gift *you* may have already received, perhaps the greatest gift of all—the gift of a gentle heart.

"...puzzled watchers reported that for no apparent reason the three meditating Wise Men suddenly and simultaneously smiled. And some observers insisted that so did the Babe."

The Little Thieves of Bethlehem

The lessons of the streets in Jerusalem were all they knew. They snatched food and clothing from street sellers' stalls. They spent their days causing trouble, and their nights in the stable behind the inn. Since they took turns sleeping in the manger, they became known as the "Manger Thieves."

Tamar, Bukkiah and Joanna, two eleven year old boys and a ten year old girl, street children from Jerusalem, had wandered down the dusty roads and camel trails to Bethlehem. In no time at all they became a nuisance—and, said some, a plague to the entire community.

Their easiest and most profitable prey were camel caravans of merchants who passed through Bethlehem once or twice a week. The travelers couldn't imagine that these three juvenile beggars, or "shnorrers" as they were known in the Aramaic tongue, could dupe them so easily without their even realizing it. In fact, one could say the children were so clever they made the travelers pay to be stolen from. The youngsters accomplished this with a simple, effective formula that seldom failed.

Bukkiah attracted everyone's attention. He danced, somersaulted and walked on his hands in the center of the caravan camp. Everyone laughed and applauded and remarked upon how supple and strong he was. Occasionally some of the wealthier and less greedy merchants would toss him a coin or two.

Then tears would flow as Joanna, in a simple sweet voice, sang songs of the heart, of lonely moonstruck deserts, of home and family—and occasionally of riches and glories to come when the Messiah would announce his presence and the Romans were driven away forever. This often brought another two or three coins that might purchase enough food for a meal or so at the marketplace.

During all this touching diversion, Tamar, smallest and most cunning of the trio, applied his talents out of sight on the far side of the camels. Deft fingers opened pouches and quickly removed food, enough to feed three small people...not so much as to be missed. Every now and then a small trinket or shawl was taken. These items brought larger dividends when later sold to someone in the next caravan passing through Bethlehem.

The townspeople weren't entirely unaware of what was happening. They knew the children were on their own, scrounging for food and an occasional garment. But everyone had his or her own personal needs, and homeless children weren't included on anyone's problem list. Men were indifferent to what they considered childhood pranks. And most women were hard put to care for their own families, let alone being concerned about three homeless waifs.

As always, however, one or two were outspoken about it. Among them were Abanah and Helah, two embittered villagers who met daily at the market and always enjoyed an hour's conversation dissecting the reputations of others. Drawn together by their disdain of everyone else, they delighted in their shared contempt. On this particular day, they had much to talk about.

"Have you heard about all the commotion at the inn?"

"You mean the light and all the shepherds?"

The women exchanged cold glances of solidified skepticism.

"Did you see the older man and young girl? She was obviously about to deliver a child when they arrived, and must have done so by now?"

"Yes—and it won't last; he's far too old for her."

Knowing, scornful glances at this exchange.

"Have you ever heard such outlandish stories of healing?"

Prolonged sighs of disbelief passed between them.

As they continued their conversation, liberally sprinkled with numerous negative, condemning comments, Abanah noticed the three children "Manger Thieves" strolling in her direction between the stalls of market vendors. Her eyes widened abruptly as she watched Tamar's expert hand dart out and snatch a handful of dates from one of the tables. The children quickly raced away before the merchant noticed what had happened.

"Those boys will end up rowing their lives away in a Roman galley," Abanah said with obvious contempt.

Helah agreed with relish, and added, "Yes, and that girl—she'll become someone's slave, or worse."

Tamar, Bukkiah and Joanna dashed recklessly through the marketplace and entered the camel and donkey auction area without being careful of their steps. Bukkiah stumbled behind a startled donkey just as the beast lashed out with his hind hoof, smashing the boy at the side of his head, leaving him unconscious, blood streaming from a deep gash. There was no sign of life in him as the frightened Tamar and

Joanna pulled him away from the busy auction area and further harm. He remained unconscious from the blow, and began to take on the pallor of death before his horrified friends.

Abanah and Helah had followed in the direction of the three children and approached closer shortly after Bukkiah's careless mishap. Though they could plainly see the boy's serious condition, such was their scorn for the youngsters that they made no offer of help. Other passersby, intent on their own affairs, paid no attention to the critically wounded boy. Furthermore, they wanted to keep as far away as possible from the detestable Abanah and Helah.

"Quick, go for help!" shouted the frantic Tamar.

Joanna turned to run, and a few steps away saw Abanah and Helah. She rushed to them screaming and pleading for their help, but the two women were terribly unkind in their refusals.

"We've no time for such as you," declared Abanah as she heartlessly turned away.

And Helah joined her, smirking, "Why don't you go to the stable behind the inn? They say miracles are happening there."

Struggling to hold back her tears of confusion and helplessness, Joanna sat on a nearby doorstep to calm herself. The world seemed so harsh and cruel, she felt, with nothing but death waiting its turn.

With saddened eyes cast groundward in despair, she noticed a small, flat pebble in the sand, brightly colored, worn smooth by sand and sandals over many years. Its beauty seemed a reprieve from the ugliness of her short life. She picked it up from the sand, thinking it might make a cheerful gift for Bukkiah when, and if, he ever became conscious.

After a moment, she recalled Helah's remark about going to the stable. "There's nothing to lose," she thought, "and perhaps there'll be help." So she headed in the direction of the inn. Several steps later she noticed Abanah and Helah following and watching her closely. "They're going to make fun, and be mean and nasty," she thought, "but I'm going anyway."

* * * * * * *

> Joanna didn't know it, but she and the three Wise Men, along with Abanah and Helah, were destined to meet at the Birthplace. Before *they* appear, as part of this story let *us*, within ourselves, visit the manger through a few moments of inner meditation.
>
> Let us offer our blessings, experience an exchange of energies, and meditate on a renewal of the birth of the Christ within, and the interconnectiveness of us all. Perhaps by then the people in our story will arrive.

* * * * * * *

The three Wise Men, Abanah and Helah, and little Joanna all arrived at the stable at the same time. The small group already present, shepherds and a few townspeople, parted to let the late arrivals enter and approach the manger. There was an expectant quietness in the air. The place was full of wonder, almost as it must have been when the heavens and earth were created. Life and vitality were present, but as a dormant potential waiting to be used rather than as an objective reality.

The three royal visitors slowly and reverently approached the crib, each leaving a gift. As they turned away, their faces seemed graced with a luminescence which reflected the sparkling eyes of the Babe. Then they seated themselves on the floor of the stable, closed their eyes, and remained motionless and silent, apparently absorbed in a mystical reverie of the Spirit.

Joanna watched closely as the gifts were offered. As did all the others in the stable, she sensed the specialness of the Babe's presence. An irresistible desire came upon her to approach the manger-crib upon which she had slept so often. But, what gift could *she* give?

Then, she remembered the beautiful stone. Suddenly confident, she stepped forward, knelt at the crib, and tenderly placed the stone among the folds of the Babe's blanket. Before she could withdraw her hand the Babe's tiny fingers clutched hers and held them tightly. Joanna closed her eyes in an ecstacy of joy such as she had never, ever known.

A few moments later she slowly opened her eyes and was startled to see Abanah kneeling on the opposite side of the crib, a single teardrop glistening on her cheek. For a few brief moments they looked into each other's eyes. Joanna sensed that some extraordinary change had occurred in Abanah, that her scorn and bitterness had turned to wonder and love. Joanna glanced at the tiny hand still clinging to her fingers and could hardly breathe as she sensed a special warmth flowing from the Babe to her. It surrounded her. It filled her completely. And Joanna thought she could see it touching Abanah, too.

At that moment, Abanah slowly reached across the crib and tenderly took Joanna's other hand in hers. As she did so, the warmth which flowed from the Babe and now filled Joanna with its presence, became stronger still surging on to engulf Abanah too. It was as though the three were actually one, caught up together in some magical essence that, with every breath, flooded them with love.

The Babe loosed his hold on Joanna's fingers, and as though from some common inner prompting she and Abanah rose in unison, walked slowly past the Wise Men, Helah, and the rest, then hurried toward the place where a heartsick Tamar was still waiting with the terribly wounded Bukkiah.

Helah arrived breathlessly a moment later with a pouch of healing herbs which, she explained, were given to her by one of the noblemen at the manger. "For your friend," he had said. She thought he was referring to Abanah, but now realized he must have meant Bukkiah.

The four of them managed to carry Bukkiah to Abanah's home where she bathed the wound, applied both olive oil and the healing herbs, then covered him warmly on her most comfortable quilt bed. An hour later he roused slightly, enough to greet his friends, now including Abanah and Helah, and even smiled weakly at his predicament.

In the meantime, back at the stable, puzzled watchers reported that for no apparent reason the three meditating Wise Men suddenly and simultaneously smiled. And some observers insisted that so did the Babe.

The three youngsters remained in Bethlehem. Among the villagers they now had friends, especially Abanah and Helah, who took them into their homes and helped them to learn better ways of life. Those two former cynics reversed their own disagreeable ways as the village busybodies and bad news carriers, and became renowned for their selflessness and readiness to help others.

In the stable, the outer evidence of the extraordinary event which changed all their lives quickly disappeared. But the spiritual atmosphere lingered on and on. The memory of that wondrous experience never faded from their minds.

They often visited the manger together, for to them it was a sacred place of special meaning—a place where each of their lives was changed. They would sit together quietly, silently, and relive its wonder and meaning, just as others also do to this very day. And, just as *you* may do, wherever you are.

"Eventually
even the
simplest act
touches the
lives of
thousands in
ways you will
never know."

Secrets of the Magi

The Magi were priests practicing the principles given them by the avatar named Zoroaster. Their name for God was Ahura Mazda, meaning Great Light. And, you remember, it was a great light in the sky which called three of the Magi to the birthplace of Jesus. During the days of 2,000 years ago, the Magi were known to possess supernatural abilities, such as seeing into higher dimensions and communing with those who peopled them.

If you were one of the Magi, a Magus, you would be able to become one with the Great Light, Ahura Mazda. One with the Divine fire, from which all power and created beings and things were sent forth into manifestation. You would be able to use that great invisible fire to heal, to learn the secrets of signs and symbols, and to read the eternal messages which the stars portrayed.

Among the dedicated followers of Zoroaster was an aged Magus named Ali Noor. He lived his lifetime in, and labored among, the poor people of an obscure village—and he himself also lived a life of poverty.

His heart was true, but his listeners were few. His dreams had been of masterful achievements, of throngs of the faithful circling his altar on which the sacred fire burned with bright and meaningful radiance. He dreamed of healing the multitudes and bringing peace to the world. But, alas, his hopes were never realized. He became disconsolate, dejected. He considered his life a wasteland, barren, desolate and harsh as the desert land in which he lived.

Therefore, it seemed quite odd to him that he was one day approached by a small boy, a pathetic urchin, obviously undernourished and penniless, a stranger to the community. And while the local villagers held Ali Noor somewhat in awe, the little one approached him without apprehension, but nevertheless with respect.

"Honorable sir," he said, "My name is Gaspar, and I wish to learn the secrets of the Magi."

Ali Noor could hardly conceal his amusement at such a startling request from one so obviously unsuited. Thinking to put the boy off, he said, "My secrets are few. You should go to the city—and there be instructed by the wisest of the Magi in the many mysteries that require years of learning and dedication."

But the youngster would not be put aside. "Please!" he implored. "More than all the sands in the desert, more than anything in the world, even more than the light of life itself, I want to be as you are and do as you do, for I feel called to a special mission."

Ali remembered feeling the same inner call when he was a young man. His heart warmed as do the desert sands in the morning sun. He took the young aspirant into his care. He found a family who would house, clothe and feed the boy. He shared secrets with him—secrets known only to the Magi. How to express reverence in your mind while gathering the sacred tamarisk for the holy altar fire. How to place the twigs upon the altar so that but a slight wisp of smoke ascends heavenward. How to impart a special prayer to the ceremony so *it* would ascend and enter the invisible, as did the slender curling smoke spire rising from the altar fire. And the symbolism of the tamarisk itself, that its delicate feathery leaves whispered of another land beyond this, where all is light and beautiful.

He taught the boy how to become one with the energies of the earth, air, water, and especially fire, for fire is the great light of the solar system and the symbol of God. He instructed Gaspar in the inner technique of lighting the holy fire.

"Within your self," he said, "adjust your mind to be open to the symbol of the flame. As you meditate upon its ever increasing light you will become one with the Great Light which it represents."

He demonstrated the Magis' many methods of healing. "This is a mixture of aromatic herbs to place upon the body of a sick person," he told Gaspar. "It represents the way in which mind and prayer combine in a holy medicine which the person takes within the body while breathing. The Magi 'heal mind and soul as well as body,' " he emphasized.

"Mix herbs with sesame oil," he said on another day, "and with a tincture of dates, or figs, or honey. Always combine elements which match your insight of a person's nature and need. Mentally kindle the healing flame within them, for all ingredients and components must unite with the Great Light to provide that Light's harmony and healing power to one in distress."

During the months that followed, Gaspar was a learner of unusual quickness and brightness, studious and enthusiastic in all his lessons. But one day the youngster suddenly disappeared and was seen no more. Ali grieved, for he had come to love the lad as a father loves a son. For him it was a son found, and all too quickly lost. But the years passed with no word of him from any source. Questioning the members of an occasional passing caravan proved futile. There was no word of Gaspar—neither tradesmen nor traveler, from village or city, provided even the slightest trace.

The old Magus, his life ebbing with the dismal passing years, finally became resigned to departing the earth. "After a life of so little accomplishment," he wondered, "what will my fate be? I fear I have earned no reward. I fear I have not kept faith with the Great Light."

In his mind, after the manner of the Magi, he decided one day to give release to those special inner elements that allow body and soul to separate, each to go its own way. And that night he experienced what at first he thought was a magnificent dream.

In his spiritual body, he rose from his physical form. He entered a great light which, after a moment, he realized was the light of the spiritual world. With hardly a backward glance at his inert body he hovered a few moments above the sands of the Arabian Desert. Then he was drawn quickly through space, westward over the mountains of Peraea and across the northern waters of the Salt Sea. Some mysteriously urgent, silent, beckoning call, drew him unceasingly onward.

His sense of urgency heightened as he hovered over a greening land of gentle hills verdant with olive trees. How different from his barren homeland. Finally he arrived at a village, and in it a stable, carved from a rock overhang, but filled with shepherds instead of cattle. There, to his astonishment, was a newborn child in a manger. Now a newborn babe is always a center of interest and delight. But as Ali looked over the shoulders of others, into the Child's face, he was filled with an extraordinary feeling of wonder and awe.

Almost endlessly, it seemed, he thoughtfully watched villagers, shepherds, and travelers from distant places, come and go. As they approached the crib with its tiny infant, Ali thought, "Somehow this appears to comfort them, relieve them of their worries and pains, strengthen their bodies and renew their minds." He listened to their hushed but excited talk of signs and wonders, of healings, of a Great Star mysteriously appearing and hovering overhead.

Silence abruptly fell upon everyone present. Three magnificently attired men were approaching the manger. Everyone moved aside to allow them entrance. Ali Noor immediately recognized them as Magian priests from afar, one of them dressed in the garb common to the Magi of his homeland.

One of the Magians, the youngest, stepped forward, and knelt at the crib. From within the folds of his robe he drew forth a pouch of the kind in which travelers carry their gold coins during a journey. Gently, he placed it at the foot of the crib, and bowed his head a few moments in silent prayer—*must be a valuable gift, Ali thought.* Ali Noor watched with intense fascination as the Babe reached out with his tiny fingers and lightly touched the hand of the Magus. The Magus then rose and took a place in the shadows behind the other watchers.

Then the other two priests, in turn, followed suit, leaving a pouch, spending a time in silent meditation, and returning to places among the others present.

* * * * * * *

Now, in your mind, stand a moment beside the aged Magus, Ali, at the manger. Engage in a silent conversation with him. Think of what you would say to him, what questions you might ask him, and what he would say to you in response.

When you've finished, return to the story and share in the old priest's wonderful experience at the crib with the Babe.

* * * * * * *

As Ali continued to observe the spiritual drama unfolding before him, he became aware of a pause in the procession of those who pressed forward to spend a moment in the Child's close presence. He decided that even though he was invisible to the spectators, and though he could not present a gift, he would approach the crib and pray for the Babe, for obviously this was an exceptional child—and, he thought, "Is not the world at all times greatly in need of exceptional people? I must have faith that one day it will be."

So he reverently approached the crib, knelt and prayed, thanking the earth for receiving into its domain a bearer of the potential for all things good and eternal. He paused. The Child's hand slowly raised again and reached toward Ali just as he had done with the Magi.

At that instant Ali's lifelong questions and doubts crept again into his mind. "What have I done to deserve the blessing of this moment...and from this child?" he wondered.

And slowly but surely, a soft voice out of the Great Silence bearing the wisdom of the ages spoke to him, "One of the noble but simple secrets of the Magi is that even though what you do seems insignificant in comparison with what someone else might do, it is important to all humankind. Eventually even the simplest act touches the lives of thousands in ways you will never know. It is like a gift of gold, for it represents divine faith, humankind's most precious quality."

Ali thought he understood, but he wasn't quite sure until a moment later. He rose from his knees, and turned toward the young Magus who had placed the pouch of gold before the Babe. There was an indefinable magnetic quality about him which Ali found irresistible. As he looked again into the face of the young man, the first vague hint of recognition began to register upon Ali's consciousness. "Could this be—was this really—has the impossible occurred? Yes! It *is* Gaspar! My young pupil! Grown and become a magnificent Magus!"

Ali was startled to realize that Gaspar could see him—recognized him—and knew his thoughts at this moment. He stared intently at Gaspar, and was certain he saw the hint of a smile appearing upon his noble face.

Then, as it sometimes wondrously happens, two worlds were united, two hearts spoke to each other. And the message they exchanged was another of the great secrets of the Magi—that the gift of gold and the prayer of faith are the same in the sight of God...but the gift of gold is of little value without the prayer of faith.

In that moment, Ali Noor knew that his life had not been in vain—that he had indeed kept faith with the Great Light. He turned and entered that Light. And Gaspar smiled again.

"But, indeed, there was an angel. A young woman, perhaps twenty, who appeared to be made of mist until she came closer. The she looked just like anyone else, except that she seemed to glow."

The Story of the First Christmas Tree

Ten year old Ann began the Christmas season in the hospital. She was terribly discouraged. She'd looked forward to the excitement of the holiday...the tree, lights, gifts, and Christmas Day at Granny and Grandpa's. But it was not to be. At least that's what the doctors said.

A mysterious blood condition had made her weak, listless, hardly able to speak. "There'll be tests, transfusions, treatment and a lot of bed rest required," said one of the physicians.

"We'll be lucky if she's ready to go home by the end of January," said another. The prospect was gloomy indeed for Ann, her mother and father, and her eight year old brother Reggie.

Ann's family made their daily visit to the hospital just the day before Christmas. Her mother lingered alone with Ann in her room while her father and brother remained in the nearby waiting lounge. It was an obvious effort for Ann even to whisper. But she put her little hand in her mother's and murmured, "I've got a secret!"

"Tell us about it next time, dear," said her mother. "You'll be stronger then."

But, weakly moving her head from side to side in protest, Ann whispered, "No! Now!" And she continued without waiting, "I've met an angel. She's coming to take me on a trip." Exhausted by these few efforts to speak, she sunk back into her pillow, her eyes slowly closed, and she fell asleep.

Ann's mom, Ellen, wiped tears from her cheek as she finally left the room and joined her husband Art, and their son Reggie, in the stark hospital waiting room. She sat beside them, shaking her head in disbelief as she told them what Ann had said.

"An angel!" Art snorted. "Now, on top of all the other complications, she's hallucinating!"

Sensing Reggie's lack of understanding, Ellen explained, "Hallucinating is seeing something that isn't there, but you think it is."

"If it isn't there," Reggie asked, "how can you see it?"

He seemed to be challenging his mother, but she was too distraught to try to explain, so she gave him that old response all children have heard, but which means nothing to them. "You'll understand when you're older."

Knowing well the futility of any further discussion on the point, and truly worried about his sister, Reggie didn't bother to complain.

As it was late, the family left the hospital for home, totally oblivious to the dramatic episode occurring in Room 402, where Ann, so they thought, lay unconscious and hallucinating.

But, indeed, there *was* an angel. A young woman, perhaps twenty, who appeared to be made of mist until she came closer. Then she looked just like anyone else, except that she seemed to glow.

"Are we going on a trip?" asked Ann. "You promised."

"Yes," answered the angel. "We're going to go see the first Christmas tree. And you may call me Alona. We're... well, we're something like sisters. I'm going to spend a lot of time with you for the rest of your life. You can go with me on this trip, but first you must learn how we do it."

"I'm ready." Ann was truly excited.

Alona smiled reassuringly. "First," she explained, "you must be very calm. Then think of yourself as walking right out of your body. Don't worry about it. I'll help you. Just do it. Come on, let's do it together."

Ann hesitated. Alona realized how unsure of herself and self-conscious Ann felt about it. "Don't worry," she said. "No one can see us."

Hand in hand the invisible couple walked along the corridor to the elevator, and out of the hospital.

"Now," said Alona, "let's try something else. We don't really need the sidewalk to walk on. Let's start walking through the air."

Ann gasped at the thought that such a thing could be done. But by now she had complete trust in Alona so, again hand in hand, off they went through the air. It was scary for Ann at first. But she soon gained confidence and they went faster and faster, Ann becoming stronger and stronger along the way.

"We're going back in time," Alona informed her. "We're going to ancient Egypt!"

Suddenly, there they were! Four thousand years ago in a small Egyptian village surrounded by date palm trees. Workers were climbing the trees and carefully taking down the dates. The rest of the villagers were preparing a celebration giving thanks for the annual harvest of the life-sustaining food.

"Is that the first Christmas tree?" asked Ann skeptically, pointing to the nearest date palm.

"Maybe," was the somewhat unsatisfactory reply. "But let's look somewhere else, too. Let's go to China."

Ann indicated her wholehearted approval by thrusting her hand in Alona's and urging her to move upward again. She seemed more confident and stronger, as though a new kind of life was becoming part of her.

So away they went—to China, three thousand years ago in relation to *our* time today. Ann was engrossed...the little girls in colorful dresses and huge hair ribbons; the people, young and old together, who seemed to be enjoying themselves as if on a picnic; the red and gold buildings which Alona said were temples, something like churches. And suddenly there were hundreds of trees with little gold colored balls hanging from their branches.

"Are these the first Christmas trees?" Ann asked.

Again Alona's puzzling answer was, "Maybe."

"They smell like oranges," Ann said.

"They are," replied Alona. "The very first oranges came from where we are right now, and they're loved here in China. But we must move on. Let's go to Bethlehem."

And away they went. Ann had no difficulty keeping up with Alona now, and in fact from time to time she rushed on ahead when she was pointed in the right direction. Clearly her strength was increasing at each exciting visit.

So—to Bethlehem, two thousand years ago. The crooked, narrow streets were filled with people. But no one could see the two invisibles. Ann was suddenly shocked to realize they were at the manger and she was watching the two thousand year old drama with the Babe, Mary and Joseph, the shepherds, the Wise Men and all the rest. Alona nudged her toward the tiny Babe. She stood there quietly a moment, awed by the significance of it. A great hope began welling up within her—that Mommy and Daddy and Reggie would believe it when she told them where the angel had taken her.

* * * * * * *

Let's pause for a few moments to join Ann and Alona (in our minds and imagination) as we, too, visit the manger.

There's the Babe in his crib. How his eyes sparkle as he lifts his tiny right hand as though waving a greeting and giving us a blessing. There's Mary on one side of the crib and Joseph on the other.

We can almost see—and at least we can sense—the great waves of love that flow between them and outward to us and everyone else in the Presence. It's a wonderful experience as its power enters heart and soul.

But we wonder about not having a gift to offer. Hardly has the thought come to mind than a "silent voice," perhaps our own higher self, speaks with assurance, "You have brought the gift of your presence, and in exchange have received the gift of the Babe's Presence. In the higher reality they are equal in worthiness. Their value is in their acceptance and their love. Leave your inner gift here, and take the Babe's inner gift with you as you continue your journey in life."

* * * * * * *

As Ann and Alona finally left to go into the street again, Ann thought that surely somewhere now she would see a Christmas tree with lights and ornaments and tinsel, but none appeared. There were lots of lovely trees, though, which Alona said were fig trees.

"Are *they* the first Christmas trees?" Ann asked.

"Maybe," answered Alona. "Like the others we've seen, they symbolize life that returns again and again. Now we're getting closer to where we really want to go," she said, "so let's don't waste any time. We'll go in *that* direction," she added, pointing a little to the right.

Ann now displayed a growing eagerness for the next experience. There was dramatic improvement in the coordination between her mind and her—well, her spiritual body, she guessed. It was no surprise to her when Alona said, "We're in the time zone of one thousand years ago, and we're in Germany."

It was obviously cold, though Ann didn't feel it. There was snow everywhere. Glistening icicles hung from the roof of the dimly lit log house they were approaching. Ann also noticed they were surrounded by a forest which she could hardly see in the darkness of the night.

As they entered the house, Ann first saw the crackling fire in the fireplace, then, at the wood stove, a woman about the same age as her mother. Ann turned as she heard the whisper of a voice from across the room, and there in a small wooden bed she saw a little girl about her own age. Somehow, Ann knew the little girl was very ill.

"Will Daddy be back soon?" the girl whispered to her mother, who simply nodded.

A moment later her daddy did appear, bringing into the house a small pine tree, roots and all, in a wooden bucket. He placed it near the little girl's bed. The aroma of pine quickly filled the house as he fastened a small candle on each branch, perhaps seven or eight of them. He lit them, and the little girl's eyes widened in awe as the warm, lovely light filled the room. "How beautiful!" she gasped. "Let's call it our Christmas tree."

Alona stepped to the head of the bed and placed her hand lightly on the girl's forehead. Ann thought she could actually see energy flow into the girl, strengthening her back and legs. Suddenly she sat up, threw back the covers, and walked into her surprised mother's arms. Both of them sobbed openly, as her daddy tried vainly to hide his tears behind a big handkerchief.

"*That's* the first Christmas tree!" Ann exclaimed.

But as usual, Alona said, "Maybe." Then she added, "Like the others, it's a symbol of life renewing itself. It stays green the year around to show that life never really dies, but keeps being reborn." Then, after a pause, she said, "But remember, we wouldn't have had *our* Christmas tree if there hadn't been other trees of celebration thousands of years ago."

"I liked *all* the different trees," said Ann.

"No matter the tree," replied Alona, "the idea is the same everywhere and for all time. It's the *idea* that's important. If people around the world would think of the idea, instead of their differences, it would help bring them together in peace. And now it's morning, and we have to go home."

In a moment Ann found herself in bed again in the hospital. Alona stood at her side, smiled, and touched her forehead as she had the little girl's in Germany. Strength surged through Ann's body, too, as her family came walking in the door to her room, and Alona's figure was fading away.

"Merry Christmas," the family said, trying to be as cheerful as possible.

Ann startled them by shouting, "Merry Christmas!" as she jumped from the bed and hugged each of them.

The family remained in astounded silence as Ann told them the story of her angel, all the places they visited, the astonishing sights they saw, and especially the first Christmas tree.

"Oh, that's *wonderful*, dear," cried her mother.

"Amazing, simply amazing," exclaimed her father.

But Reggie had a question. "Sis," he asked soberly, "on these trips, did you get to see any football games?"

Ann for a moment put on her most grownup demeanor. "Reggie," she admonished, "you'll understand when you're older!"

"Strangely, Uzziah began to experience again the warm surge of love that had enveloped him the night before. It was like the warmth of the sun suddenly appearing from behind a cold raincloud."

The Wealthy Beggar of Bethlehem

In his youth, Uzziah was a strong, handsome young man for whom life seemed to hold abundant promise. Fate held a different view of the matter.

He had lived with his parents in a small village a short distance south of Bethlehem. One day a marauding band of Amorites swept out of the wilderness of Judaea and raided the village. They left his father dying and kidnapped his mother, probably to sell her to a traveling caravan on its way to other lands with slave merchandise to barter.

Uzziah had the further misfortune to have been clubbed in the head by one of the raiders in the struggle. His face was left with an ugly scar, and his sight dimmed halfway to total darkness from the terrible blow. His soul was wounded, too. The loss of his parents, coupled with his own misfortune, created an acid in his mind too strong for his spirit to overcome. The visible scar on his face was not nearly as great a disfigurement as the invisible scar within.

For a time he was cared for by his father's brother, but the day came when that arrangement could no longer continue and he had to go into the world on his own. He became a tattered, wandering beggar, finally making his way to Bethlehem.

For years he maintained the basic, essential relationship between body and soul by ransacking trash heaps, occasionally cleaning a stable, and begging from the more lenient caravan travelers. He hoarded as many as possible of the coins given him through the years. In time, so skillful was his begging, he became secretly wealthy. But he was always fearful that someone would take his wealth from him, so he kept up the appearance of poverty by accepting the task of cleaning the stable at the inn. His wealth, however, was no antidote for his continuing inner sickness.

Uzziah had no friends. It would be an exaggeration to describe his existence as meager. It was as barren as the desert sands. The more restricted it became, the greater his bitterness. In fact, outwardly profitable though it may have been, inwardly his plight was fruitful soil for resentment that grew stronger with each passing caravan, as his troubled mind dimly recalled the beginning episode of his misfortune.

There was a well near one of Bethlehem's gates, and not far away an old deserted hut which had become his home. He kept busy begging. The grotesque scar on his face became his fortune for it aroused the pity of all who beheld it. It seemed to Uzziah that he was gaining a measure of repayment for his disfigurement by asking tribute, in the form of alms, from wealthy travelers whose caravans paused overnight in the town.

Near dusk one evening, he heard the faint sounds of an approaching caravan. His practiced ear told him it was an exceptionally small one, and at first he thought he wouldn't bother leaving his hut to ask for alms. However, the metal trappings of the camels' harness had an unusually expensive tone and decided he would try to add to the two sacks of gold, silver and copper coins he had begged and hoarded over the years.

Uzziah hurried toward the well and saw three obviously wealthy, weary travelers dismount their steeds. They went immediately to the well and busied themselves splashing water on their dusty faces.

"Perhaps," thought Uzziah, "while they are not paying close attention, this is my opportunity to obtain a truly great sum of money to make up for the shame and loneliness I've suffered for so many years."

Deftly he slipped his hand into the nearest saddlebag and withdrew a pouch which, his experienced touch told him, contained gold coins. He quickly hid it in the oversize pocket of his ragged galabeya and boldly approached the three travelers at the well. He had recklessly decided to extort as much from them as possible.

They paused in their libations and conversation to look at him silently for a moment. Uzziah thought to himself, "Let them get a good look at my scar and perhaps they'll be prompted to give me more coins."

They made no such offer. It seemed to Uzziah that if it were possible to look *through* someone that was what they were doing to him. Finally one of them asked directions to the inn. Uzziah knew the inn was filled, but he had become so uncomfortable in the presence of the strangers that he wanted only for them to be on their way. His nervousness was heightened by the pouch of gold in his pocket. It seemed to become heavier each time one of the travelers looked him steadfastly in the eyes. He wished he had run the moment he had taken the pouch. He silently pointed in the direction of the inn, turned and walked toward his shack, hoping to get away from the strangers. He anxiously, greedily, wanted to examine and count the contents of the stolen pouch. But fate was to change the direction of his footsteps.

One of the travelers moved swiftly after him, clapped a hand on his shoulder and spun him around. Uzziah trembled in fear that his thievery had been discovered, but the stranger gave no sign of knowing about the beggar's crime.

"Will you not accompany us to the inn?" asked the stranger. "We are not familiar with the way through the village."

Uzziah's first thought was to run, but to avoid suspicion he deemed it wiser to comply with the request. He headed toward the inn, the strangers and their camels following single file through the narrow, winding streets. It was then that he first noticed the strange, soft light that seemed to be glowing just beyond the inn. It grew brighter as they approached—and as the shadows lessened Uzziah noted an unusual number of townspeople, and also shepherds from the countryside, all slowly heading in the same direction as if drawn by some unknown but irresistible force.

When the travelers arrived at the inn, Uzziah motioned them to the door but they made no move to enter.

"On to the light," said one of them.

"Yes," added the second, somewhat impatiently. "On—on to the light!"

Uzziah still hesitated. The third traveler, the one from whose saddlebag he had removed the pouch, exclaimed, "To the light, and we will give you something worth far more than gold!"

That promise, spoken with such authority and certainty, was compelling to Uzziah—so he accompanied them to the stable where a mother and father hovered over a babe in a crib.

Uzziah watched, awestruck, as one of the strangers approached the Baby, bowed low for a moment, whispered a few words to the mother, then placed a small pouch alongside the crib. He recognized the unmistakable aroma of frankincense. The second stranger did precisely the same. This time the aroma was of myrrh.

The pouches appeared to be exact duplicates of the one he clutched so tightly at that very moment. A demoralizing thought struck Uzziah. Had he stolen the very pouch intended as a gift for the Babe? Did the stranger know he had it hidden in his garment?

The third traveler, the one whose pouch Uzziah now concealed beneath the folds of his galabeya, instead of approaching the crib, looked so intently at him that he thought the fire of his gaze would burn him to a crisp. Surely the stranger knew what he had done. He was unable to move a muscle. Unable to speak a word. It was as though he was suspended in some time warp in which the eyes of the world were fastened upon him, could see him and knew his thoughts.

* * * * * * *

Traditionally, according to legend, only the pure in heart ever approached the Babe in the manger. It seems to me that such a view is unrealistic. Everyone has the potential for purity, but the practical reality is that none of us have completely objectified that ideal.

Perhaps we actually approached the Babe in that long ago day. But if we do so now merely in spiritual fantasy, the fantasy of inner reality, let it be with an open heart of pure intent. In the magic of your mind, stand at Uzziah's side in the center of that moment of eternal mystery—the birth, or rebirth, of an experience that helps you become more than you are.

* * * * * * *

Suddenly the intensity in the stranger's gaze softened. The world began to move again. Uzziah was never able to tell exactly what happened. For the first time in many years he felt a warmth of love that saturated his entire being. Without any hesitation, or reservation, or remorse, he withdrew the pouch of gold from its hiding place in his garment and held it out at arm's length. The stranger nodded, and the hint of a smile flickered a brief instant on his face as he took the pouch and placed it with the other two in the crib.

A wave of relief flooded Uzziah's mind as he continued to watch others approach the crib and leave gifts. He did not join them for he had no gift to give. Or so he thought at the time.

Hours later, through the now nearly deserted streets, he returned to his hut. The thought of sleep was as far from his mind as Bethlehem was from Rome. He noticed that the first light of dawn was touching the sky when, once more, he heard approaching travelers. It was the three strangers again.

They stopped and asked for information about the caravan routes to the east. They were particularly curious about those which were the most arduous and least traveled. Uzziah had listened to so many caravan travelers' stories through the years that he could tell them exactly which way to go. He gave the information and a few moments later they were on their way.

Hardly had the sounds of *their* leaving died away when the other principals in the magic scene he had witnessed the previous night came into view—the mother, father and the Babe. They, too, made inquiries, but of routes toward the *west*, toward Egypt.

As he spoke with them, strangely he began to experience again the warm surge of love that had enveloped him the night before. It was like the warmth of the sun suddenly appearing from behind a cold raincloud. With the feeling came an impulse he could neither explain nor resist.

He hurried into his shack and from a small wooden chest drew two sacks of coins—his entire fortune. He pressed them into the father's hands, and over his protests said, "But the way is long, and expensive, and you will need special provisions for your family." He nodded meaningfully at the mother and child.

Finally the gift was accepted and the travelers were soon merely a memory. But it was a very special memory. It was not only in his mind, as memories mostly are. Mysteriously, it was in his heart. It was throughout his body. Yes, it was even in the horrible scar he had worn so many years. Wondering, he put his hand to his face and touched the livid, welted streak. It seemed softer...and smoother.

After a few moments he sat on the rough-hewn threshold of his hut and pondered the experience over and over. He wasn't sure what to make of it. The knowing and the not knowing were coupled and wrestling in his mind.

For just a moment he wondered if he might have played a part in some historic event that would be meaningful to others. After musing on the possibility he quickly dismissed the thought as far too improbable to consider. Surprisingly, the realization that he had given away his only possessions of value—his two sacks of coins—somehow didn't seem to disturb him at all.

A wide smile, his first in many years, erupted on his face. Without really knowing why, he spoke aloud to himself. "I haven't a copper to my name, but I am the wealthiest beggar in Bethlehem."

"Do not dismay.... You may think the cross is lost, but it is not. It's spirit is still in your heart. And, after all, the spirit is really the cross—the object itself is only its physical form and vehicle."

The Story of the Christmas Cross

William Bridgestone was a craftsman in wood. His artistry was the envy of every cabinetmaker and woodcarver in the city. But, his life was troubled.

His son, Paul, anxious to seek his fortune on his own in the world, had traveled to another city. No word had been heard from him for more than two years.

Even worse, one year at the holiday season, his wife, Celeste, had fallen seriously ill. She struggled courageously. She even tried, though unsuccessfully, to do her usual Christmas shopping and giving. Finally her strength completely failed, and she died. Heartache and loneliness were William's only heritage, as he moved from the home he had shared with Celeste and Paul to a modest apartment in another area of the city.

Though he had little spiritual understanding of his own, he recalled from time to time the ideas his wife had discussed with him, particularly those about life in the higher world. And though totally unreligous himself, he decided that in honor of his wife he would carve a small wooden cross to carry with him in her memory.

The result was a work of unsurpassed beauty—small, delicate and intricate. He poured the love of his heart into it and carried it with him wherever he went. Perhaps he imagined it, but he always thought that Celeste's presence was close by when he touched it. There was a special feeling about it. It seemed mysteriously to have a life of its own. And this is the story of the way that hidden life was born and reborn into the lives of others.

It was five days before Christmas, that mystic moment of the solstice when the sun decides not to forsake the northern hemisphere and to be born again into the northern skies. William was on a long and lonely walk in a strange section of the city, thinking about Celeste—and with ever increasing frequency about his son, Paul. He was passing a church when, for some unaccountable reason, he was prompted to enter and sit quietly in the sanctuary for a few moments.

He took the cross from his overcoat pocket and looked upon it fondly. In the dim light it actually took on a soft and tender glow. For a moment he thought he felt Celeste's presence next to him. He placed the cross on the pew beside him and became totally absorbed in his thoughts of her and of his missing son. Finally he rose to leave, absentmindedly forgetting the cross.

It was dark as he walked down the front steps of the church, and on the next to last step he stumbled, sprawling to the sidewalk. Though he wasn't injured, his age caused him to rise slowly. A passerby strode quickly to his side to offer help, taking him by the arm to steady him.

"Are you all right—are you hurt?" he asked.

William's startled mind went almost entirely numb with disbelief as he recognized the well-remembered voice of his son. They shouted and hugged each other in joyous recognition. In their excitement they hardly noticed the sobbing figure of a woman entering the church behind them.

After more than an hour of happy reunion, William remembered the cross and hurriedly returned to the church to retrieve it. But it was no longer on the pew where he had left it.

The only person in the sanctuary was the woman, still sobbing softly, who had slipped past during the unexpected meeting with his son. He thought it would be rude to interrupt and ask if she had seen the cross, so he turned quietly and left. Somehow he was not at all depressed at the loss of the carving, for the reunion with Paul more than made up for it, and he had the feeling that Celeste was reassuring him that it wasn't really lost but was on a journey of its own. Little did he know that at that very moment it was clutched in the trembling hand of the sorrowing woman.

She had been wandering aimlessly in total dismay at a turn of events which threatened destruction to her husband's career and the welfare of her entire family. He had been accused of embezzling a huge sum of money from his employer's business. In truth, he had been loyal and dedicated for many years, and had not taken the money, but he stood accused and his trial was to begin the next day.

At the thought of his being unfairly imprisoned, a great fury began to arise within her. As it became a raging inferno, she was tempted to throw the cross violently in the direction of the church altar—when something stayed her hand. She pondered the cross for a moment, and remembered that at one time a cross bore the body of one who was also falsely accused, but who was finally liberated.

Gradually her rage subsided until a feeling of peaceful resignation to the circumstances calmed her consciousness. She sat quietly, almost motionless, for a long time, perhaps two hours, occasionally marveling at the pulsing sensation of life that she felt radiating from the beautiful carving which she continued to hold.

Suddenly she was startled to hear her name shouted, like a clap of thunder, from the rear of the sanctuary. She turned quickly to see her husband dashing down the aisle, calling at the top of his voice, "It's over! It's over!"

When he finally calmed himself, he poured out the story of a miracle. Within the last half hour his employer had been to their home. He brought the news that a co-worker, a man of steely hardness and cold disdain for others, had an unbelievable change of heart and had just phoned to confess that he was the culprit who embezzled the money and was ready to pay it back! The false accusation was therefore dropped! There would be no trial!

Now sobbing with joy instead of grief, arm in arm, the couple walked through the front door of the church. At the steps they were accosted by an obviously drunken beggar, an old man who, in a surly voice as unpleasant as the scent of cheap wine that was all about, demanded a handout.

The woman realized she was still clutching the cross and, impulsively, placed it in the outstretched, expectant hand of the beggar. Shocked at not receiving any money, he stared at the cross for a moment in disbelief. He looked up at the church door ignoring the joyous couple completely, put the cross in the pocket of his ragged overcoat and staggered inside. He entered the sanctuary in a stupor, stumbled half way down the aisle, slumped into one of the pews and fell asleep.

Or so it seemed.

True, he was unconscious outwardly, but in his mind a remarkable vision was transpiring. He was living an inner life in a time of long ago. He was a shepherd, watching a flock by night, and puzzling over a solitary brilliant star. It was so dazzling that in its light all other stars in the heavens dimmed and disappeared from sight. He watched it gleam like an enormous jewel displayed on a background of dark blue velvet.

Then, from the center of the star, he heard a voice, saying, "Go to the stable beyond the village inn, and there witness the birth of him who is with you always."

"Religious tommyrot," he thought, but in his vision he simply had to obey, so he set out immediately to follow the instructions. On the way he was asked for guidance by three foreign princes who unaccountably seemed headed for the same destination. In fact, they arrived sooner than he did and when he came to the manger they were leaving gifts before a babe in a cradle. Without knowing why, he felt compelled to do the same.

From a large pocket in his shepherd's shirt he withdrew a crude cross that he had fashioned only the day before. He had copied it from an emblem he had seen among the Essenes, though he was not a member of that order. He placed the token close to the crib. A great light burst from it and its radiance seemed to bond both him and the Child in a mystical oneness that surpassed time and space.

In that oneness, though he heard no voice, a startling message flashed into his mind. "There is," it said, "a great rearrangement of the energies which surround the earth. All the elements of life are now being brought together in a new combination within you. A combination that supercedes the normal level of consciousness in the human individual and becomes, instead, a Consciousness of the Divine. In this higher state of consciousness there is naught but joy, love, health, strength, understanding, wisdom and all the purer properties which are significant to you: new birth, new consciousness, new vitalization."

* * * * * * *

As it requires some time for this intricate message to be absorbed into the old man's waking consciousness, spend a few moments reflecting on the meaning of the message voiced to his inner self.

What energies are penetrating his normal consciousness? What changes do those energies create in his waking mind? What are the changes in his attitude? His personality? His view of life and his place in it?

* * * * * * *

The vision slowly faded into darkness. Consciousness gradually returned to the old man in the pew. He grasped the cross in his coat pocket, and it seemed that boundless strength surged from it into his entire being.

He rose quickly and left the church. His steps were no longer faltering; his countenance reflected a curious, and at the same time courageous, combination of joy and determination. Simply by looking upon him, tattered garments notwithstanding, one would know that here was a person who set his course in life and was going to follow it with perseverance to a successful culmination.

When he arrived at the cheap hotel room which he knew now was merely a temporary stopping place, he was dismayed to discover that along the way the cross must have slipped through the large hole in the pocket of his ragged coat.

"Will everything I've gained in the last few hours now slip away from me?" he asked himself. Apprehensively, he sat down to ponder this critical concern.

As he became quiet, another voice began speaking to him. Oddly enough, it seemed a voice from the past yet at the same time a voice from the present...a voice from far away and at the same time very near...a voice that was supernatural and at the same time very natural. Though he did not know it, it was the voice of Celeste, in whose memory the cross had been carved.

"Do not dismay," she said. "You may think the cross is lost, but it is not. Its spirit is still in your heart. And, after all, the spirit is really the cross—the object itself is only its physical form and vehicle. Its symbol.

"Soon after it slipped from your pocket, it was found by a little child whose home was in ruins and who needed its strength just as you once did. And it will continue to go from hand to hand, and heart to heart, wherever it is needed.

"Its spirit, which you now possess, is enhanced and multiplied by everyone whose life it enters. And each person who touches the cross finds that it is not really a symbol of death, but of birth...a birth into a new dimension, a birth of a new and glorious consciousness."

The voice ceased. And the man understood.

Is it possible that Celeste had done her Christmas giving after all?

You and I are not privileged to hold the Christmas Cross in our hands, except in our imaginations. But we, too, have the spirit of it in our hearts, which amounts to the same thing, for everything we imagine has its own form of reality. We know that the story of the Christmas Cross, in a thousand different ways, is a story in each of our lives, and it is a story without end...for it is reborn every year.

"Thus far Eliakim has chosen to align himself with the negative energies of the circumstances of his life. We often do the same, as a matter of choice, conscious or unconscious, until it becomes habitual. The habit can be broken."

Eliakim's Gift

This is the story of Eliakim, who had been orphaned when his parents, Joseph's dearest friends, died during one of the fever epidemics that plagued the land at intervals. Joseph had taken the destitute lad into his home and made him an apprentice in his shop. He was soon impressed with the young man's intelligence and reliability.

Eliakim was eighteen, and extremely bright. However, he was also extremely cynical. Some would say, for good reason. During his parents' illness he had prayed daily for their recovery, with deep conviction and sincerity. However, it was one of those inexplicable times when his pleas brought no response whatever. The experience left in Eliakim's heart an obstinate bitterness that could not be softened, even by Joseph's understanding and sympathetic attention.

Eliakim decided that for the rest of his life he would have nothing to do with prayer, or religion, or compassion in any form. Yes, he appreciated what Joseph did to help him. "But then," he reasoned, "I give him a good day's work and he is nothing out of purse for teaching me the trade."

On the day he learned of Joseph's betrothal with Mary, Eliakim's bitterness flamed to new heights. First, he had himself secretly hoped that one day he might claim the beautiful young girl as his own. Second, the pride of his young manhood was deeply wounded that a man as old as Joseph would capture Mary's beauty and charm, leaving him destitute in heart as well as purse. He reasoned, and frequently told himself, that probably when the betrothal was consummated Joseph and Mary would insist that he leave the household. He would then have to find living space elsewhere, quarters sure to be cold and barren, for he could not afford anything equal to the comfortable place he now enjoyed.

Then one day a remarkable series of events began to unfold. At the well, Eliakim heard that Mary was with child. Actually he was not displeased at the news. "Perhaps," he thought, "Joseph will now put her away privately somewhere, and my place in the household will be secure."

Later that same day Joseph, who had for some time obviously seemed troubled, closed the shop somewhat early and told Eliakim that he wanted a few words with him, for he valued his opinion. "Possibly," he said, "you can help me clear my own thinking."

"Ah," thought Eliakim, "I'll help him clear his thinking for certain!"

He wasn't really ready for what Joseph was going to say.

"You know the problem I face," he began.

Eliakim nodded, anxious for the opportunity to express his view that Mary, according to the custom, should be sent away.

Joseph continued, "I'm not only faced with the conflict between my heartfelt feeling for Mary and the custom of our time, there is also another aspect I must consider."

"This is even better than I hoped," thought Eliakim.

"I've had a troubling dream," said Joseph. "It seemed as though one of Jehovah's very own messengers appeared before me and assured me that even though I continue with Mary I need not fear any social consequences. But even more than *that*," Joseph spoke slowly and emphatically, "I was told that the soul of the child partakes more of the Holy Spirit than any other being ever before born on this earth! What do you think of such a dream?"

Eliakim at first thought of choosing his words carefully. He was amazed at the extent of the impression the dream had obviously made on his benefactor. But the seeds of his own experience had so deeply rooted in his consciousness that he cast caution aside, and replied, "Except for those whose minds are unstable, dreams are for women and children. They mean nothing. And even to consider that such a dream as yours is a Divine spiritual event is the height of ignorance—even idiocy."

Joseph gave no sign of the deep wound the words of his friend's son had inflicted upon him. But Eliakim was unable to hide *his* dismay when Joseph stated his firm belief in the dream and its prophecy that a son would be born with the full imprint of the Divine upon him. He announced that he would follow the proper ceremony, consummate the relationship with Mary, and she would be his wife.

In the months that followed, bitterness and animosity grew like twin souls in Eliakim's heart. "It is sheer folly," he thought. "All these preparations for the birth of an insignificant child. Now if it were the child of a princess, or a queenly monarch, perhaps it would be justified. But in this case..." His thoughts trailed off into the impracticality of it all, at least from his point of view.

Then came the news that they must journey to Bethlehem for census and taxation. Along the way, Eliakim was distant and at times even unfriendly, especially toward Mary. But neither the heat and dust of the journey, nor the coldness of a now openly hostile friend, affected her patience or sweet disposition.

Then—the Birth. Due to the hardness of his heart, Eliakim was unimpressed.

The shepherds—with his usual condescension Eliakim was unimpressed.

The star—as it didn't seem too visible, Eliakim was unimpressed.

The visiting dignitaries, the Magi—Eliakim was unimpressed. He deliberately refused to offer the Babe a gift, as all the others had done.

* * * * * * *

Before continuing this story about Eliakim, this is an excellent time to make a connection with the subtle energies of the past. Thus far Eliakim has chosen to align himself with the negative energies of the circumstances of his life. We often do the same, as a matter of choice, conscious or unconscious, until it becomes habitual. The habit can be broken. Frequently a step at a time, or occasionally in a single stroke.

In a meditative mode, see if you can sense a lingering vibrational chord of the birthplace and birthtime during which the Nativity was recorded in the *Book of God's Remembrance*, the Akashic Records of that event. Its spiritual atmosphere still persists as a vibrational accent in primal substance. Let it mingle with your own thoughts and feelings of that long ago moment. Savor its joy, its sweetness, its majesty. Then continue the story.

* * * * * * *

The day after the Magi suddenly disappeared, Joseph told Eliakim his second dream—that he should take the Babe and Mary and flee to Egypt to save their lives and, "Perhaps," he said, "to fulfill the ancient prophecy—'Out of Egypt have I called my son.'—a prophecy which might indicate that in Egypt, the land of ancient wisdom, the Child will mature in understanding and spiritual knowledge."

Eliakim was again disdainful to the point of total disrespect. He criticized Joseph for their intended journey and refused to accompany his benefactors to the land of mystery and promise.

It was the next day that the soldiers of Herod arrived on their murderous mission, and discovered that one among their quarry had escaped. However, Eliakim was pointed out to them as a member of Joseph's family and was consequently arrested. There remained just enough self-respect and loyalty in his heart that he refused to inform the soldiers of the direction taken by Joseph and his family. He maintained having no knowledge of their destination. For his allegiance he was sentenced to a lifetime of hard labor in the forests high in the mountains of Lebanon.

As the weeks, months and years went by, there slowly drained from Eliakim the last residue of resentment which once had hardened his heart. Perhaps it was the exertion enforced upon him. Or his musings in the darkness of countless silent, lonely nights. Or the grandeur for which the mountains were noted. Or a cup of homesickness for his former friends. Or perhaps a combination of *all* these. But one night there pulsed within him an irresistible urgency to escape—and an opportunity to do so. He seized it, and decided to make his own way to Egypt and, if possible, find Joseph, Mary and the young boy, to make amends for the way he had treated them.

Little did he know that on that same night Joseph experienced his third prophetic dream. "Take the young Child and his mother," said the figure which appeared to him, "and go into the land of Israel."

So Eliakim traveled south from Lebanon while Joseph, Mary and Jesus traveled east and north from Egypt, directly toward each other and an unexpected encounter. It is in the wilderness of Judea that the final episode of our drama occurs.

Joseph and his family were warily passing a lonely Roman sentry outpost, manned by only three or four soldiers. They were stopped by the captain of the guard who began informing them of marauders in the area. But suddenly he stopped short, studied Joseph intently for a moment, trying to recall where they might have met. Then...he remembered.

"You're the head of the family that escaped us when we raided the homes of Bethlehem for male children!" he snarled.

Joseph could only stand petrified at the realization that the instructions of his dreams, the lengthy flight to Egypt and the return, may all have been in vain.

Even as the captain spoke—was it chance or the result of Divine destiny?—Eliakim came upon the group and realized in a moment the awful seriousness of the situation.

"Yes!" shouted the captain as he sighted Eliakim. "You were there, too. We arrested you, and this Child should have been killed along with the others."

He took a threatening step toward Mary as if to wrest Jesus from her. At nearly the same moment Eliakim leaped into action. He realized that he, and he alone, might create a sufficient diversion to save his friends. "You'll never arrest me again," he growled, then added enough insults to arouse the full anger of the soldiers. Quickly he turned and ran off the roadway toward a distant outcropping of rocks where the soldiers would have a difficult time tracking and capturing him.

"After him!" called the angry captain to his men.

In less than a moment the soldiers were gone, leaving Joseph and the family to hurry aside in the opposite direction and find safety and shelter.

They spent the entire night in prayer for the safety of the one who, in a brief moment, more than repaid the debt he owed—and in thankfulness for their own deliverance. When Joseph finally found a few moments of sleep, it was troubled, and again he dreamed. He seemed caught up to the Most High and was told to change the destination of their journey from Bethlehem to Nazareth.

We do not know Eliakim's fate, although it seems likely his last moments on earth were at the point of a Roman sword. We do know that he overcame his doubts, and that although he had offered no gift at the Christ Child's birth, in the moment of crisis he offered himself without hesitation. Is there any gift greater than oneself?

And that he exemplified the qualities of loyalty and love. Are not loyalty and love among the finest of personal qualities?

And that he made it possible for you and me, and our families and friends, to learn the lessons and share the joys of this Holy Nativity Season. Are not learning the lessons and sharing the joys of this season the most memorable gifts any of us might receive?

So Eliakim has indeed given a memorable gift to each of us.

"And so it was, with that unique interactive capacity possessed by twins, that Janet and Jeremy dreamed the same dream that night, simultaneously—a dream of the third angel..."

The Three Universal Angels

This isn't a story about three specific, biblically named angels, such as Gabriel for example. Nor the type of angel often seen on television. This story is about a special *energy*—a spiritual energy abundantly present in every angel. It's about three special varieties of this energy which every angel possesses.

And, for that matter, they're present everywhere else, too. That's why I refer to these three important variations of angelic qualities, or energies, as universal angels.

Actually this story is about a homeless girl and boy. They were twins, named Janet and Jeremy. They lived in the center of a large city, in a leaky, distressed plywood shack. It was a place sarcastically referred to by its residents as Emptyville. That name simply meant that everyone who lived there was practically penniless, hopeless, and had to occupy makeshift "houses" of cardboard, cracked corrugated plastic, rusty tin and other castoff materials...flimsy shelters that could easily be rebuilt when destroyed by man or nature. And it often happened.

Janet and Jeremy had been orphaned runaways about a year, and being very intelligent for their age had managed to obtain a shack and make it their home. A bond of similar circumstances and misfortune integrated the residents of Emptyville into a special society in which most everyone either helped everyone else, or helped themselves to what everyone else had. In the grip of desperation, few could really be trusted.

Once in a while, Janet and Jeremy would become very discouraged about their situation. Bright as they were, they could see no improvement in the future. They were too young to get jobs.

But their sharp minds made the best of their circumstances in the creative way which is common to many. It was Christmastime, so they played the game of gift giving. They would walk downtown, gaze in the store windows, and fantasize about giving each other the gifts on display.

"I give you that ski parka," said Janet one day close to Christmas as they stopped to look at a store window display of mannequins on skis.

"Thanks, Jan," Jeremy pretended surprise and pleasure. "And I give you that pair of skis."

Jan matched Jeremy's feigned appreciation. "Great! I'll use them on my vacation up north."

They knew very well that a ski parka in Emptyville would invite envy at the least, and possibly even violence. And skis were of use to them only as firewood. In spite of using their vivid imaginations, keeping warm in a make believe parka and skiing on a snowy slope far from Emptyville, it wasn't easy to avoid reality completely, and finally it captured their attention as the two trudged forlornly back to the pitiful place they were obliged to call home.

Of the two, Janet was the more creative. She possessed a wellspring of intuitive thoughts that were constantly flowing through her consciousness. Jeremy was the practical thinker whose logic was greater than his years.

As they neared Emptyville, Janet broke the silence. "I have an idea, Jer," she announced. "There's something we really can give each other for Christmas. Tonight, let's see if we can dream. Then in the morning I'll give my dream to you by telling you what it was, and you give yours to me in the same way. That can be our Christmas gift to each other."

Jeremy didn't think much of the idea. He thought of a gift as something substantial which one could see and hold and use. But to please Janet he agreed to try.

The next morning, Jeremy recalled a vivid nighttime vision, so real he couldn't believe it was only a dream. However, he hesitated to tell Janet for fear she wouldn't believe it. On the other hand Janet was eager to share her dream, too, and couldn't wait to relate it.

"Jer, I dreamed of an angel." This statement alone jostled Jeremy's thinking about his own experience. Janet continued, "This angel told me that her name was Faith, and that we should have faith that our lives will change—and that some day we'll really have some of the things we've been pretending to have. What do you think of that?"

Her question had a triumphant air that was a challenge to Jeremy to believe—and to let his practical mind accept the experience she described as a promise of the future. She thought of it as a Christmas gift that would be welcomed. She was surprised when Jeremy told her he had his own dream to describe.

"Jan, I don't know if there is such a thing as a man angel, but I think maybe one came in my dream. He was a big man, and strong. I liked him. He talked to me a long time. He said, 'Jeremy, I want you really to succeed in life. There is one thing you must always remember; you may be a little afraid now and then, but you must always be courageous. There may be some things you think you cannot do, but you must try. I'm always close to you, and you can always call on me for help.' Then he told me that his name was Courage! Jan, that's my Christmas dream gift to you."

Both Jan and Jeremy were excited about their dream gifts. They discussed them for a while, then decided they should share them with the rest of the residents of Emptyville wno had always helped them wher in need. So, early on this cold, drizzly Christmas night, they visited from shack to shack, telling their unusual experience, and how everyone could use the angels' message to escape from Emptyville. Most everyone who listened at all was polite enough, but didn't seem to share their enthusiasm for the experience...or the message.

"Two angels? A woman named Faith and a man named Courage?" They listened out of politeness, but obviously didn't believe something that extraordinary could actually happen.

The twins didn't realize how difficult it is for those who have suffered so much to accept as real the incidents they were describing. So it was only natural they would be disappointed and discontented, thinking that their efforts at helping their friends accomplished nothing. They returned to their shack, thinking of it as a hiding place from the indifference of the others.

They sat quietly in the semidarkness, eyes closed, holding hands as if to help each other accomplish something very difficult. It being Christmas Eve, they wondered what Bethlehem was like on that night so long ago.

A state of reverie, a dazed reality that was both fact and fantasy filled their minds and they agreed they were indeed in Bethlehem, visiting the manger. They discussed the fact that they seemed to be on a mystical journey—that they were there, yet they were not there.

They even discussed that the Babe was whispering to them, saying, "Do not worry; you will understand. Many who will visit with me through the years will still feel this strange melancholy that you feel. They have yet another lesson to learn."

Being twins, it's understandable they might both "hear" the same words—words that seemed to surround them rather than being spoken to them. The hint of tears that shimmered in their eyes was only an indication of inner joyful tears in the heart that were the mark and symbol of understanding.

* * * * * * *

> If you would like to join Jan and Jer in their special Christmas journey, close your eyes a moment, and in your imagination join hands with them as you drift back to the Birth that changed the world. Perhaps an important personal message will enter your consciousness too. Possibly an understanding of a lesson meaningful to your life will be revealed to you.

* * * * * * *

Just as suddenly as they made their mystical journey to Bethlehem, they were back in their plywood hut. And that night another idea sprang into Janet's mind! "Let's try another experiment," she said. "Let's see if we can dream the same dream together, at the same time!"

And so it was, with that unique interactive capacity possessed by twins, that Janet and Jeremy dreamed the same dream that night, simultaneously—a dream of the third angel, the angel of Love. In the dream they realized that faith and courage aren't quite enough—that those two qualities, as fine as they are, really need help from the angel energy of love.

They realized they needn't have felt so despondent. What they did through faith and courage, and what they tried to do for others, may not have produced outstanding results immediately. But the important element that made it all a complete whole was that of love. And just as surely as they knew this truth, they had found a way out of Emptyville.

Now as you and I consider Jan and Jer's dream, do we not realize how accurate it was, and still is? Does it not reinforce our own realization that *Faith* and *Courage* really need *Love* to complete the picture of the angel of all angels? And that *that* may even be the greatest discovery of all humankind.

I really don't know what happened to Janet and Jeremy. I'm sure that throughout their lives they treasured their gift of sharing, their visit with the Babe in the manger, and their visit with the Three Universal Angels—Faith, and Courage, and Love. And I'm certain they must have asked, and received, the presence of those Special Ones on countless special occasions. Does it not follow that the rest of us should do the same?

"You are all the characters, for you are in the nature of the One Spirit that embraces us all. And for all of us, our fantasies either reflect or create our realities."

Epilogue

"An epilogue," says one definition of the word, "is a concluding section at the end of a literary work, often dealing with the future of its characters."

This epilogue is intended to serve that purpose by discussing *your* future—for you are not *one of*, you are *all of*, the characters portrayed in these Christmas stories and meditations.

You are all the characters, for you are in the nature of the One Spirit that embraces us all. And for all of us, our fantasies either reflect or create our realities.

It's my belief that each of us possesses a spiritual nature which we should preserve, nurture and exercise from time to time. I also believe that doing so is a creative process, allowing each of us our own unique experiences. May you find this work a refresher and reinforcer of your own inner spiritual essence. Sensitize it to the healing and support it receives daily from the higher dimensions, enabling the Christ Spirit to be reborn in you and yours. That Spirit awaits you each time you visit the magnificent manger within.

* * * * * * *

The publisher of this book is a nonprofit organization presenting metaphysical, mystical, philosophical and self-help material. For more information write:

Astara Administration Building
792 W. Arrow Hwy.
Upland, CA 91786